© Vanessa Krchova 2024

Thank you to my sweet friend, copywriter Lucy Everett for proofreading this book.

ISBN: 9798884071810

To you, dear reader,
thank you for your
curiosity to hold
this book.

> HEALING IS THE CAPACITY TO HOLD THE PAIN, RATHER THAN GET RID OF THE PAIN

Before I start sharing my journey with you...

Working with plant medicine and what we experience during this time, is greatly connected to how we are at the moment. No experience is ever alike. The medicine doesn't work as Western medicine - when you feel a headache - you get painkillers for the headache - to cure the symptom and feel a relief. Whereas, with plant medicine it goes into the cause. And healing doesn't necessarily mean immediately feeling better; healing is the capacity to hold the pain rather than get rid of the pain. And funnily enough, when we're able to consciously and lovingly hold the pain, the pain transforms, after a while, because we take its power away.

Very often 'the healing' starts way before we actually work with the medicine, the process we experience - the way we decide to experience this, is part of the healing itself. Therefore, I found it important to share how the medicine came to my life and my time prior to actually physically working with it. And so, I have divided this book into two parts.

Part one - my time leading up to the retreat.
Part two - my time at the retreat itself.

I invite you, during the time of reading this book, to put aside any expectations of how this book will make you feel and to read it with an open heart, and mind, to the infinite possibilities of being.

With much love and gratitude, let's get started shall we?

xx

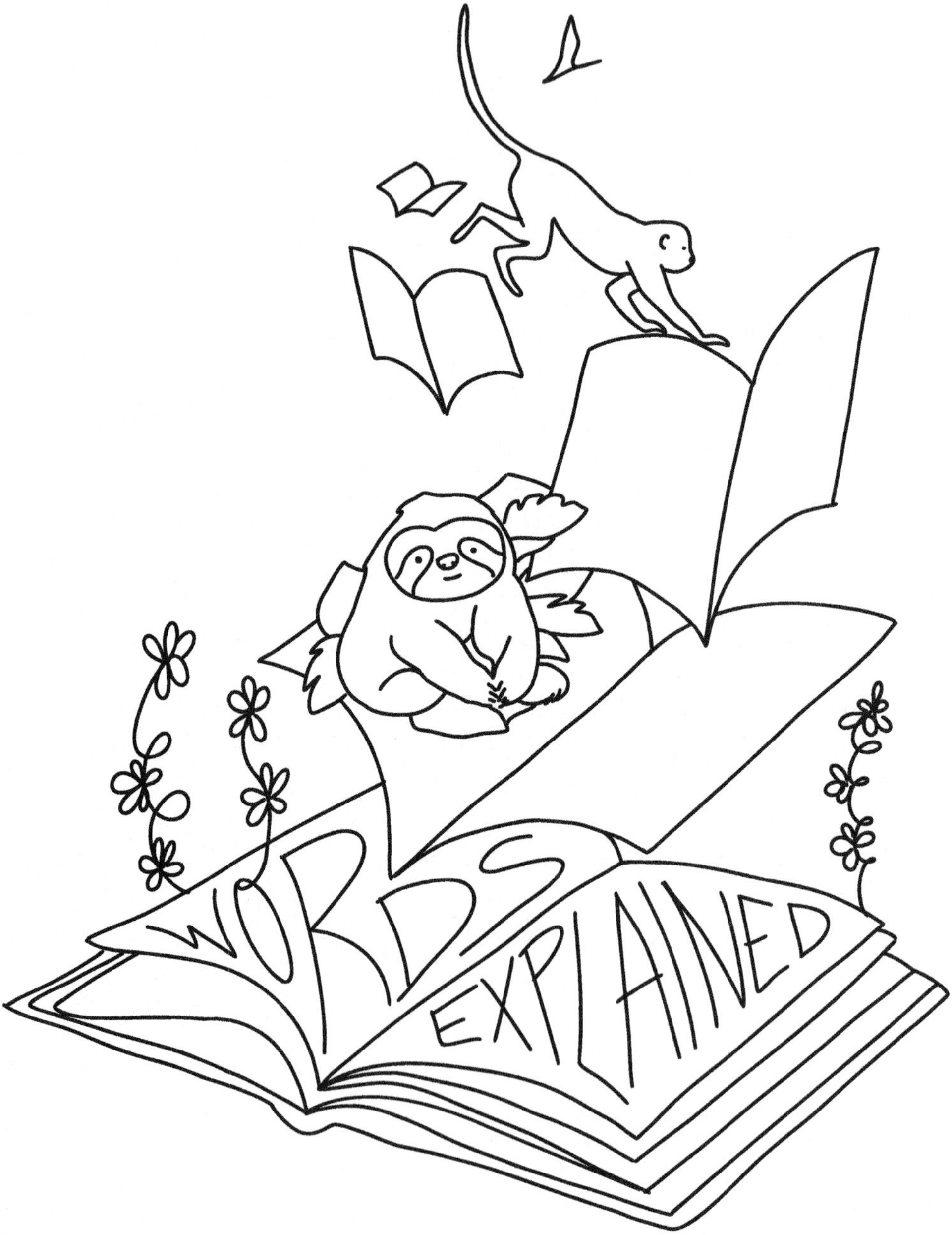
WORDS
EXPLAINED

When you first see one of these words in the book you'll find a * next to them to remind you to come to these explanations should you need them.

Temple Of The Way Of Light;
short: The Temple

A traditional plant-medicine shamanic healing centre located in the Peruvian Amazon Rainforest that offers intensive ayahuasca retreats with female and male Shipibo healers.

Ayahuasca;
short: Aya

It's one of the most powerful and well-known natural entheogens known to man. The name ayahuasca comes from Quechua, a widely spoken South American language found throughout the Amazon: aya means 'soul' or 'spirits' and Ayahuasca means 'vine.' The full name, therefore, means 'vine' of the 'soul' or 'vine of the spirits.' It is a powerful plant-based medicine that can open a doorway to communication with the inner worlds and spirit realms.

Shipibo

The Shipibo culture, originating along the Ucayali River in the upper Peruvian Amazon, is well known for shamanism. The Shipibo are one of the few cultural groups that have managed to maintain their language, art, and mystical plant medicine in this region of the Peruvian Amazon. They have a particularly strong relationship with ayahuasca, and many consider the Shipibo to be the most highly skilled shamans in the Peruvian Amazon.

Maestro

Maestro is the Spanish word for 'teacher.'
It is the title given to those who have achieved a level of mastery with ayahuasca and other plant medicines.

Curandero

A general term for a healer in Amazonian plant traditions. Literally, 'one who cures.' The term is not exclusive to plant medicine healers, though it is commonly used in this way.

Dieta

Dieta is the Spanish word for 'diet.' The dieta is to be followed in order to prepare not just the body but also the mind and soul to incorporate the healing energy of ayahuasca. Following the Ayahuasca diet also shows the spirit of ayahuasca one's intention and is a test of discipline and commitment.

Ikaros (singular ikaro)

Ikaros are traditional indigenous Amazonian songs that are performed as accompaniment to sacred plant healing ceremonies. They are musical prayers that embody the powers of spirits of plants and animals, deities, ancestors, and elemental forces. The songs are channelled into this reality by the healers.

Purge

The release of energies, which is often associated with ayahuasca and other plant medicines that cause one to expel (known as purgatives). Common types of purges include vomiting, diarrhoea, sweating, coughing, temperature changes, yawning, laughing, crying, and psychological release.

Maloca

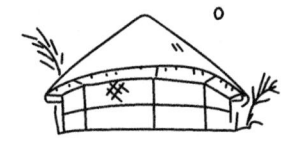

A traditional round Amazonian building with tall, conical-shaped thatch roofing built in an open-air style with mosquito netting around the perimeter. Malocas traditionally function as community gathering spaces. Ayahuasca ceremonies are held here.

Tambo

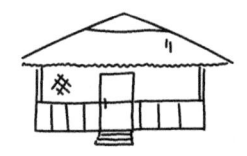

Name for a jungle hut in the Peruvian Amazon rainforest. Tambos vary in equipment and sizes. Ours were built out of wood and had mosquito netting instead of actual windows and doors, and each consisted of a bed, hammock, toilet, sink, a few shelves, and, importantly, an oil lamp.

Mapacho

Sacred tobacco. A local, wild variant of tobacco native to the upper Amazon. Mapacho is commonly used as a medicinal plant and is widely utilised as a complement to ayahuasca ceremonies and healing.

Camu Camu

A sour berry, native to the Amazon rainforest, similar to cherry in colour. Camu camu is considered a superfood – mainly due to its high content of certain nutrients and powerful plant compounds, including vitamin C.

Aqua de Florida

The Spanish word for 'Water of the Flowers'.
Also known as Spirit Water. This water is made of alcohol and flower extracts and is used in South America by shamans for cleansing during ceremonies, rituals and healing processes. It's used to clear heavy energy around the body's energy field, for blessing and as an atmospheric bottle for space-clearing in rooms.

PART 1.
BEFORE THE RETREAT

Arriving in Peru

I have finally arrived in Peru. This visit has been in my heart for the last four years, I think since I visited Bali at the start of 2020. At that time, I wasn't sure why I wanted to come or what to do during my stay (as I prefer the 'not for tourists' way.) Yet, I knew one day in the near future, I would come here.

Already from the plane, just before landing in Lima and then on my last flight to Iquitos (a Peruvian town near the jungle), I felt it. I felt so much peace (and trust me, flying is not my thing), so much grounding, and like I had visited this place before. My soul already felt so familiar with and at home in this land. Understanding the bare minimum with my Duolingo level 1 Spanish and being a blond-haired, blue-eyed white girl, all the 'superficial odds' were against me feeling at home. Yet, I did.
I'm in Iquitos at an Airbnb now, preparing for the Ayahuasca* retreat that starts in 5 days. I finally got to sit down and begin to write this book. I've been avoiding it for a while and facing the resistance that usually appears before creating the project we know we're meant to create. No matter what the project is. It's us stepping into the unknown - being outside of our comfort zone - which often brings up old fears, doubts and stories. The ego is playing its tricks - testing how ready we are to expand our comfort zone and to do what we feel called to.

Facing this inner ego voice gracefully, I say:

"Thank you. I see you. Thank you for testing me - showing me my old fears, making me think if I should be somewhere else, making me wonder what people will say about this or if they will even read it. Thank you. I see you, and I choose to stay with my soul's calling; I choose to sit in my warm, sunny room with a beautiful view, and I choose to write."

This is what Ayahuasca has started slowly bringing into my life since the day I decided to work with her - clarity, so much clarity on what to do. Without pressure, without neediness or wanting or trying too hard. Simply knowing this is what shall happen right now. And so be it.

How it all started

During Covid, I made a huge move (for me). I moved from London to an area called Devon in the south of England. The whole way it happened is probably for another book; however, to say the least, it was not planned at all. Yet it was exactly where I needed to be. Over the following three years, I have healed a lot of my inner child wounds through working with different teachers, attending online courses, being in relationships, and spending a lot of time in nature. One of the biggest shifts in my being happened when I reconnected to the profound truth of my life's purpose. The knowing that the primary purpose of every human being on this planet is simply to be. It's being exactly who we are at our core. It might sound so profound, so simple; see how it sits with you, when you read it a few times.

Your primary purpose in this life is being here.

That's it! From this state of being, everything else is cherries on top of a cake.
For me, realising this and starting to connect to this awareness every day felt hugely liberating and motivating. Because I didn't need to try to be anyone else or have a title to give my life meaning. With the title, I mean literally any title we humans often like to give ourselves to give our life meaning. Designer, doctor, mother, dancer, coach, PhD, carer, artist, musician… all of these are beautiful, secondary purposes, and they can blossom very well in our lives if we've recognised our primary purpose. I AM.

I used to do/study/create things while in the back of my mind, I thought:

"When I do this, then my life will have meaning."

While working as a graphic designer, I started studying health coaching because I really wanted to help people. I really, really, really wanted to be the person who helps people because then I will mean something and feel I am making a difference in the world. Forgetting that my own presence, the way I show up and what I say in every single moment of my life can actually help people. There is absolutely nothing wrong with being a health coach; however, the place I was coming from wasn't healthy.

It's not what we do but who we are while we do it that gives life meaning and makes it fulfilling. And from this place, Ayahuasca (further on Aya) came into my life.

I am not someone who has worked with plant medicine before. Neither did I smoke much weed, or tobacco or took recreational drugs. I have done all of these very occasionally during a short period of my life, wanting to experiment and try something I haven't tried before. These behaviours weren't a form of escapism for me. Alcohol was, going to the gym was, food was, work was, living lives of the ones in the TV shows, movies and books was. All of us have our escapisms at some point in our lives, or all the way throughout. Even the most 'healthy' behaviour on paper can become escapism if we are attached to it. If the need for it becomes more important than being in the present moment and open to evolution.

Deciding to work with Aya has been the opposite of escapism for me. It's not 'doing it' for the fun of it, to 'see patterns' or to escape the world I live in right now.
I had decided to work with Aya to look within, to face all the escapisms and fears I've felt during my life that are still with me, and to transform them. So, I open up to the next version of my being and share this openness with the world in a way I feel called to one moment at a time.

It's not what we do, but who we are being while we do it that makes our life fulfilling

December '23 - The decision

I first found out about Aya around 2016 through one of my personal growth mentors Nicky Clinch, who had worked with the medicine. At that point, I thought, well, this is definitely not for me. Yet somehow Aya stayed in the back of my mind. From 'no never' became 'one day, maybe'. At the end of December, during a post-Xmas Eve chat, a dear friend of mine shared her experience working with the medicine. As she was talking I felt this weird feeling in my gut. Little scary, quite uncomfortable, yet also knowing - shit, this is what I am meant to do. This is the next step in my journey. Not because of her experience, but because of what it brought up in me.
The fear of trusting something 'bigger' than myself. The fear of trusting the spirit/God/universe - no matter what you'd like to call this essence. I know it's here, I know it's part of me (and each one of us) as well as outside of me - in everything and everyone around us.

I don't believe there is one God separated from us, who I should look up to for decisions, follow their rules and ask for forgiveness of my sins. To me, that's the need of society to look up to someone, to have a leader and to follow. God is an essence within all of us; it's our highest vibration; it shows up as guidance, intuition, and gut feeling; it's our soul. And when we are still enough, we can hear it and act upon it. All of us can.

Often when I hear it I am afraid to trust it. I begin this internal roller coaster with myself questioning if this inner guiding voice is there. And that is the second voice - the ego. The one who questions everything, who often likes to make it hard for ourselves, who throws these blocks under our feet. It's very often the second voice, the one who asks:

"Really, you really want to do that?"

So, the fear of trusting my soul and letting the ego rule has driven me to say, yes, I will work with Aya.

To be honest, at that time, I might not have been as clear about it as I am now. How it showed up for me was in the form of a relationship. I dated someone who was around during the Covid lockdown and then left to go back to his home country. For me, it was more than a Covid romance. However, I didn't want to admit it to myself and, of course, not to him, until much, much later. He had still been in my heart in an uncompleted way, in a 'maybe one day again'. Another one of my escapisms - fantasy.

I knew I wanted to clear this way of being, and I knew working with Aya would help me to transform this.

---

[1] Using futureme.com - a website where you can send yourself emails to the future. Which I do all the time to hold myself accountable or to remind myself of a certain feeling. And I highly recommend :)

Almost right after the chat with my friend, I decided to talk to a couple of people who had held ceremonies in the UK to start putting it out there. Yet neither felt right, it didn't feel like an experience I would like to have 'over the weekend'.

"When you decide to do this, do this properly. (Do it for you)."

I told myself. And 'properly for me' meant taking time off and going to Peru. Working with local indigenous tribes in the land this medicine comes from, because I believed it'll make my experience even more impactful. There are many ways and places to work with the medicine, and it's up to all of us to tune into what feels right at the time and situation we're in.

I am a world traveller; I love seeing new cultures and feeling the vibrations of places, so for me, it was a triple win to work with the medicine in this way. I already had a place in mind - The Temple of the Way of Light* (further on The Temple). It was a place where my old mentor and a few others I knew of had done their medicine work. Doing a little bit more research and looking at the Temple's website, I felt safe. I felt like 'these guys' were taking it seriously. However, they get booked up very much in advance, and when looking in January, the retreats were booked up until May. Which was giving me some extra time. Work-wise, as a graphic designer, I had recently signed a part-time freelance contract with an agency and I didn't want to leave. I didn't have a cover for my other clients, and I just started working on a very nice illustration project with my brother. The time wasn't right yet.

Some of my mentors, including myself, would question this -

"Is the time ever right?", "Am I just avoiding risking it?".

There won't ever be a perfectly paved path filled with flowers and mango trees that we can walk on without making any adjustments to our lives, that's for sure. However, we can try to force something to happen or we can flow with what life gives us, listening for the cues and letting it happen at its time. When we are truly honest with ourselves, we know if we're avoiding something or if we're being patient.

So, at the start of January, I sent myself an email to be received in July[1] to reconnect to my calling. If I still feel this way, if the calling is still present with me, I'll book my trip as my b-day gift and take time off in December. This will be much easier regarding work, as it's often very quiet between X-Mas and New Year's and I'll want to spend time in a warm country anyway.

Leading up to the trip

In the lead up to July, I noticed myself talking about a trip to Peru as a fact. Yet, I didn't mention to many that my intention was to work with Aya. When I met some new people who had worked with the medicine, I didn't want to ask much about their experience; I was worried their stories would affect my decision. What if they say don't do it? This is me - I don't want to watch the trailer before seeing a movie, so the story doesn't get spoiled. A little side note - in case you're thinking of working with the medicine - this will not spoil your experience because every experience is completely unique, and I'll definitely encourage you to follow your soul and go for your calling.

There were also others' fears that popped up when I did share what I'd like to do there. "Wow, I really admire you wanting to do this, are you sure?", "Oh, I heard it's quite a deep experience; I couldn't do it, ever."

I knew they meant well, yet it did make me a little insecure. There was a part of me that started chickening out. Thinking, well, my life is going pretty well. I'm comfortable. Maybe I don't need to. One of the things I learned in Devon was being comfortable with what is.

However, it's one thing to be okay and grateful for what is. And another is being open for growth. Not from a place of needing it, wanting it and forcing it. From a place of natural expansion. Evolution is our natural state. We are meant to constantly grow and evolve; the moment we stop, we stagnate, become unhappy and often turn into more addictions and escapism. Evolution often comes with being uncomfortable. No one ever grows in their comfort zone, in any area of their life and my life was becoming my comfort zone again.

EVOLUTION IS OUR NATURAL STATE

THE MOMENT WE STOP EVOLVING, WE BECOME UNHAPPY AND OFTEN TURN INTO ADDICTIONS & ESCAPISMS

July

Only a few days after I received my email reminder to connect to my intuition - see where I am with it, and book my trip, life sent me a very sweet sign. I went camping with a few people I didn't know, and one of them had worked with Aya in Peru. He had been there for a while, even volunteering at a retreat. So, I decided to let go of my fear of spoiler alerts and shyly asked a few questions. Just hearing him talk about his experience, I knew.

My initial plan was to travel a little bit around Peru before or after the retreat to 'make the most' of my trip. Little catch I only found out when he was talking about it - there is quite a strict dieta you are on before, during and after working with Aya this way. I looked at Temple's website and as I started reading more into it, yes, there it was: no caffeine, no alcohol, no salt, no spice, no dairy, no cold drinks, no fizzy drinks, no pork, no red meat, no processed foods, no refined sugar, no cocoa, no fermented foods, no sex (even self-pleasure), no street drugs, no other plant medicines, very little oil.

This is due to a few reasons; some are scientific - there are foods containing compounds that don't do well when interacting with Aya. Another is so our body can be cleared of any other energies and we can be as pure as possible to receive the healing and information from the plant. By letting go of these foods and experiences for a while, we also show our respect and commitment to the plant and our own healing.

I was not so worried about the diet, as I eat pretty well. Caffeine, sex and fermented foods were, for me, the 'deepest' concerns. My main challenge was how I was going to travel like this. Travel for me is hugely connected to food - it's a way to get to know the culture and I love exploring different foods. How will I be in Peru without having Peruvian cacao, coffee or ceviche? And in general, going to places and asking for no salt, no oil, no spice in every place I go to felt very limiting and no fun at all. I asked my friend if he'd travel before or after the retreat and what places he would recommend. Reading his beautiful list, he said he would advise me to travel before the retreat, as after, I'll want some quiet integration time. I started looking at some options. However, it all quickly became a bit overwhelming. Thinking I would love to see it all, but it just doesn't feel right at all.

There I had it, Aya brought it to me again - so much clarity. If you want to do something 100%, focus on that 100%, then move to the next thing.

"This trip won't be about travelling as you know it. It will be about connecting to the culture in a different way. You can travel more in Peru the next time."

I told myself and applied to be one of the attendees at the Temple of the Way of Light Retreat.

You have to fill out quite a thorough questionnaire about your mental, emotional and physical health - this made the whole trip much more credible for me and made me feel committed already. My application was approved a couple of days before my 34th B-day - it started getting real, real. And I mean on all levels...

The moment we sign up for a transformation we're in it. We show life we're ready to expand into the next version of ourselves, a new vibration. Life will then start presenting us with situations to help us clear all the residues of old vibrations and test us. To see how ready we truly are.

Yes, we could question this:

"Would these things not happen anyway?"

Well, we'll never know. I only know that any time I have committed to my growth and signed up for a course or event, life has changed. And I am one of the thousands who can say this.

The shifts that started happening

One of the biggest opportunities for growth for me has been my relationship with my family. There were still bounds between the four of us (my mum, dad, brother and me) that were not in the, let's say, 'highest alignment'. From my perspective. How I see the form of unconditional love.

These issues bubbled up, no kidding, about three days after I filled out my application and completely escalated just a day before my b-day.
Without going into the details of my family's drama, I'll only tell you what shifted in me after this.

I realised I really don't want to be involved in 'creating stories' about people, analysing all the possibilities of "Why did they?", "Why didn't they?" and "Who did what when?". It's not my vibration anymore.

It also became clear to me that as neutral and non-sided, I like to be in any argument (in the family or in the world); there will be a time when I'll have to take a stand. My stand is that I stand for love, unattached love.

Love that sees through the stories, through the mistakes we all make. Love that sees the good in people, the little innocent child we all once were. Love that sees the trauma we can act from, if the trauma is not healed. Love that is peaceful, caring, companionate, clear, honest, authentic and unattached to an outcome. Love that says "no, thank you" if it's needed.

It hasn't been easy to act from this place, especially not in this situation, and I haven't always come from this place since. Yet, it is my new standard. Whenever I don't know,

I try to take time and remind myself of this state.

One could argue that this is an impossible way of living. All I can say is there is nothing to lose from trying it. From my short experience and the experiences of others who live in this vibration, it is very possible, and it is where humanity is going. It's either this or to stay in our suffering. We always have a choice and my choice became clear.

What also became clear to me was that a lot of people don't know this form of love, because they haven't experienced it. And we can not authentically share what we haven't experienced or what we don't believe in. That's why the ones who have experienced it (or strongly believe it exists) are here. They're here to pass it on, to share it, and to help others believe it and feel it.

The way to awaken a lovelessness in people is to love them until the love within them remembers.

August

Going inwards

We were given loads of materials from The Temple to read, reflect on and set our intentions. Anytime I started reading, I felt grounded, clear and at peace. I thought it was still such a long way until my trip, but as the process started already, I decided to set my intentions; they can always change later on. Here are a few that I had at that time:

- Heal unhealthy attachments.
- Stop running away from the responsibilities to create the future on this earth.
- Open my heart to a committed relationship.

My biggest 'fear' was not the journey itself, but the integration.

"How am I gonna come back from this trip?"

I was pretty certain nothing would look the same. When I practise shamanic drumming for a couple of hours, I can be 'spaced out' for a few days, similar to a cacao ceremony or an energy-healing work I had done in the past.

The Temple supports the interaction with check-in calls, yet I still thought, what if this won't be enough? However, I also knew the fear was not going to help. It will only attract what I am afraid of even more. Of course, it'll be hard, when I tell myself it'll be hard.

What if this time it will be different? What if this time I'll come back fully grounded and certain I am here and I know what I am meant to be doing next? Because that's what the energy of Aya has brought to my life so far.

"Let me start believing this vibration." I told myself.

September

Nothing in our life happens by accident. As if there is this invisible GPS that is guiding us and every 'detour' we think we have made is actually the direction we were meant to go. This applies to meeting people, getting new opportunities, attending courses, reading books, listening to songs, and anything that comes into our lives. And so it was with this new practice called Quantum Flow I started following. Would I be open to it hadn't I signed up for Aya? Again, I don't know, and I'll leave this wonder in the universe.

As it has often happened with great things in my life, I don't even know how I found out about it. Yet there I was, practising this 3-day Quantum Flow challenge, listening to 'this man' JuanPa (who developed this practice) explaining the basics. I felt something had shifted; after the 3 practices - I felt inspired to write, I was open to sharing with others and reconnected with the intuition in my body. So, I signed up for a 14-day immersion and later on to be a certified practitioner. Not necessarily to be a practitioner but to understand the practice more, because it ticked all my boxes. It's a combination of breath and movement working with our nervous system to release our limiting beliefs and bring what we envision into our lives. It's simple (not easy, because you do go through a lot of shifts), and you can practise anywhere. For me, this was a jackpot, because in the back of my mind - I was thinking - this would be a great way to integrate working with Aya. As I'll be spending some time after the retreat in Iquitos to settle, get ready for the flight, and face 'my everyday life' again, this will be a great tool to have. Anytime, anywhere - breath and body is with me.

The entire practice of Quantum Flow and everything it has brought to my life is a long story. However, I'd like to mention a few shifts which have deeply affected who I am now, going into the work with Aya.

Healing my sexual energy

For me, sexual intimacy with a man has always been about a deep connection. However, I have not always acted this way. I had one-night stands or was in a random 'friends with benefits' type of connection. I let it happen, yet it wasn't my truth. I was scared to stand for my truth because I felt the odd one out. Because 90% of society around me sees sex purly as pleasure.

Don't take me wrong, it is a great pleasure, yet it comes from the heart. It's a heart connection first, then pleasure. When we come from the place of pleasure first, we often come from the unhealed traumas in our lower nervous centres. Sexual intimacy, with myself or a man, became very sacred to me, and I stopped being afraid to admit it.

So the 'no orgasm' part of the Aya dieta, which at the start felt like it'll be one of the hardest ones to do, feels absolutely ok right now. Very beautiful, actually, because as I am not dating anyone at the moment, it feels like my body will be purified from this old way of being, and will be ready for something new with the alignment of my values.

Healing my relationship with abundance

I started truly seeing and feeling what a gift it is to be alive. I am. I am here, I am alive, and therefore, I shall treat myself well. I was being stingy even on small stuff, on affording berries or vegan chocolate or paying for an Airbnb, when it was clearly the best option. I had stopped this. I had stopped watching every little penny that went out and worrying about it. I use money with gratitude for the service or product I'm buying, and I tune into it if it's in alignment with me and my values to buy it. And I trust that money will come back to me when I am in this alignment.

Otherwise, as has happened before, I ended up losing money or needing to use it for unnecessary repairs. Money likes to be moved, "use it; otherwise, you'll lose it."

Because I value people and services, I believe that my services are valued in the same way. We attract the energy we vibrate and when we treat ourselves small, we attract small things. We all deserve the 'crème de la crème of life' and it starts with treating ourselves this way. Interestingly, the retreat at The Temple was the most expensive one by far, and I did not second guess it at all; I knew that I was not saving on, for sure.

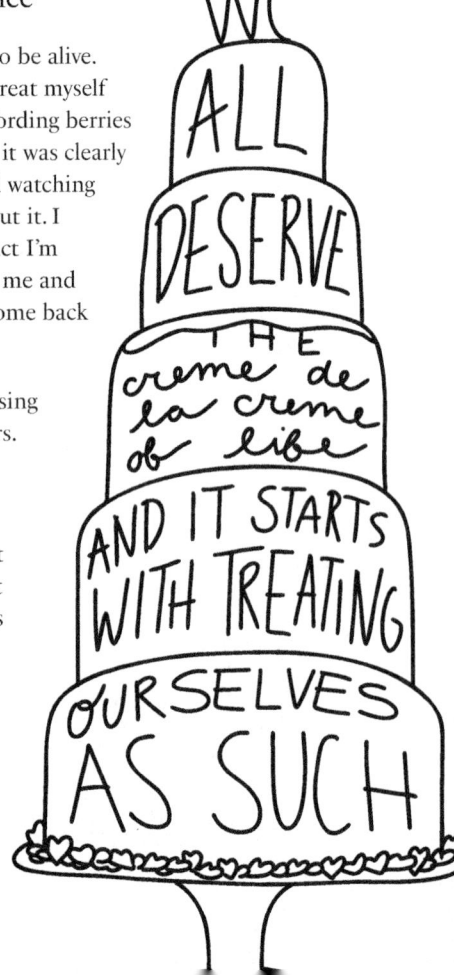

We all deserve the crème de la crème of life and it starts with treating ourselves as such

Feeling the difference between fantasy and vision

I've always loved to dream and envision how life could be. We have to become the vibration we want to attract and envisioning it is the first step. The next one is embodying it, feeling it with every cell of our body. Acting from a place as if we already had what we envisioned. The next one is starting to take action. It's the action that differentiates vision from fantasy.

Sometimes I stayed in the fantasy because I was too afraid to take action. I would rather stay in the dream than try it and risk failure. Yet, what I did not realise until recently is that trying is never a failure. It moves us forward. And when it doesn't work, it means it just wasn't for us. It means that there is something even better.

Now I hold visions of how I would like my life to go and take inspired actions towards them every single day. The rest is not only up to me. Living life is a co-creative process, a dance with the universe.

Through these shifts, life presented me with an opportunity to have an in-person conversation and beautifully end my 'one day maybe' type of relationship - the one that inspired me to work with Aya that I talked about at the beginning.

Looking at my main intentions in my journal:

- Heal unhealthy attachments.
- Stop running away from the responsibilities to create the future on this earth.
- Open my heart to a committed relationship.

I realised these were either already completed or are happening. I've healed my unhealthy attachments with people; I am committed to creating the future on this earth by being committed to my own healing and growth and sharing it with others. And, my heart is open to a committed relationship. All before physically working with the medicine...

October

Taking everyone in

From the start, I felt I was not doing this only for me.

In the world of quantum science, it's a fact that any action, any thought we have, has an impact on our humanity, on the vibration of the universe. The healing we do ourselves impacts 7 generations back and 7 generations ahead.

I knew this work was for me as well for people around me - my family, my friends, people in my energy field, people whose lives I have touched on some level. I'm not exactly sure how; they might feel it through this book, through a conversation they have or will have with me. The 'how' doesn't really matter for me. What has been important for me was the intention and knowing that as much as this is for me, it's also for everyone else. Feeling this so clearly, I realised I must share more about it - something that is often outside of my comfort zone. And that's when the calling to write this book came to me. It was a thought that gave me goosebumps, after a meditation, while making my dinner I heard it so clearly:

"Regardless of who reads this or not, your responsibility is writing and sharing your journey."

Before this moment, I kept it quite quiet amongst close friends, very conscious of whom I shared it with. I didn't feel ready to face people questioning it or commenting on it in any other way than a supportive one. There was also a judgmental part of me that thought they wouldn't get it. I assumed their answer before even giving it a try. However, the commitment and clarity that this trip was right for me became so clear that I felt rooted enough to 'risk it' and started sharing my plan with others.

IT'S OUR RESPONSIBILITY TO SHARE OURSELVES

THE WAY PEOPLE REACT AND TREAT US HAS NOTHING TO DO WITH US

I've also come to a fundamental realisation, that the way people react and treat us has nothing to do with us. It's a reflection of where they are in their life. A reflection of how they treat themselves.

It's an inner child wound, to think their behaviour is our fault or has anything to do with us.
It's understandable; when we were kids, everything in our little minds and hearts was about us. We internalised everything, and when our parents/teachers/adult figures reacted (or didn't) in a certain way, we immediately made it mean something about us. That's where all of our 'not good enough,' 'not wanted,' 'not seen' and... and... and... patterns come from (unless they were very clear, we have nothing to do with it, and it's their 'stuff'). Yes, it's possible, but I think humanity has 'some' more healing to do until all of us always live from this place. The deeper the connection, the harder it is to separate what's ours and what's someone else's. We can consciously heal this inner child wound, because it's not serving us anymore and has become emotionally mature. We feel rooted enough and know ourselves enough to say to ourselves:

"Hey, thank you for showing me what's mine and what's me. I am in my flow and I let you be in yours."

This was a great opportunity to 'put this new way of being' and understanding people to the test.

December

Preparation

My flight was on the 19th, the retreat started on the 26th, and I knew I wanted some preparation beforehand. To set everything up for coming back smoothly. I was between being excited, exhausted, a little bit scared, and so ready.

Part of me wanted to just close my Mac and leave, yet I knew there was some 'business' to take care of, especially around work. I had to find someone to cover my freelance projects while I was away and hand it all over. There was also more new work still coming in: "The last thing before you go, could you please." I'm always grateful to get freelance gigs. At this point, I was wondering how I manage it?

On top of which the dieta* had started. I knew no caffeine would be the hardest for me. I used to drink one cup per day, in the morning after my morning practice of quantum flow/run/swim or yoga. I made myself a cup of coffee with pure soya milk to start the day. It was my morning hug, my 'ok and now let's do this'. I was telling myself I was not addicted to this; I could stop anytime... yet, I didn't. I was a little bit bullshitting myself that it doesn't do anything to me; it's just one cup, I could have a decaf, yet, I didn't.

On paper, it's one cup of coffee, but I was attached to it, especially to what it did to my body. When I had coffee, I didn't need to eat until lunchtime. I had this drive to get stuff done, and I didn't want to lose it. Sounds like a little addiction to me, doesn't it?

But it was time to drop this one too. I started earlier than the 2 weeks before the retreat (which was 'the official time' to start the dieta), so I could still have some in case I really wanted to. Or I could have some cacao. Cacao has a very different effect on me than coffee - it relaxes me, opens my heart, and gives me energy in a very different way. It was not the same, but I thought if needed, I could have a treat before cutting caffeine completely. And I did have a few cups of pure cacao before the official dieta started, as a smooth transition to no caffeine times.

In the end, it all became manageable, and it all went smoothly; however, it took saying some 'nos' to meet up with people I would've likely met up with otherwise - I was reminding myself why I was doing this and what my focus is right now.

When it got real real

It was my last working day; I handed over the work I needed to do, talked to and saw people I wanted to and had a weekend of preparation at my home in the UK in front of me...

"And now what?" At that moment, I thought "S*it, this is really happening. Now it's really real; I am doing this thing, working with plant medicine, something I thought I wouldn't ever do. I have no clue what will happen, and it feels scary and great at the same time."

I was with it for a while, enjoying this moment of nothingness and surrendering to the unknown. Then some of my coping mechanisms kicked in to avoid staying in this unknown feeling for too long - I made myself extra dinner, scrolled around on social media for a while and convinced myself I must clean my fridge and the entire flat on Saturday, so everything is sparkly for when I come back.

To my surprise, the weekend went really peacefully. I was grounded in my cleaning, went for a walk to my favourite place on Dartmoor, met up with one of my close friends, packed with a little bit of resistance, as that's never been my thing, and made calls to my parents and my brother.

I felt ready. The one thing I was a little bit afraid of, was actually the time before the retreat. I had booked to stay 5 days in Iquitos - a Peruvian town near the jungle where we'd be picked up by a bus and then hop on a boat to start our journey to The Temple.
I wanted to adapt, get over the jet lag, see at least a tiny bit of Peruvian culture and spend time preparing, writing this book, drawing, and just being with myself. I also wanted to have fewer distractions than I would have at home.

I was looking forward to my chill time. However, it was over the Christmas period, and some of my friends were questioning: "You'll be spending Xmas on your own?", "What will you be doing there on your own?" I didn't question it until they did. And I will admit, it made me doubt my choices for a moment. Especially because I knew Iquitos was quite a busy town, and even though I found a pretty peaceful Airbnb with a river view, I wouldn't be in 'my comfort zone' - which for me is nature and a quieter place.

Gratefully, I went back to my lesson from before. What is really my fear here, and what is someone else's opinion and projection? And I was clear again.

Christmas has changed a lot for me. I used to love it. I was in it, all the gifting, listening to the songs, shopping, visiting, and eating; I would travel back to Slovakia,

where I am from and spend time with my parents and my brother. In the past three years, I have stayed at home in Devon. Firstly, due to Covid and later, the idea just didn't feel right; it felt overwhelming; there was too much drama, too much materialism and an unnecessary rush. For me, this time is about slowing down and reflecting on the year; it's about compassion, care, support, unconditional love and togetherness with people, and staying in Devon was bringing this up more.
It's funny I am sitting here on my own, on the 24th of December, which, in Slovakia, is 'The Christmas' (more important than the 25th), writing, feeling comfortable, filled with love, grace and peace. Knowing that this is exactly where I am meant to be and I wouldn't rather be anywhere else at the moment.

When we are comfortable with ourselves and fully comfortable with the present moment, we are never really lonely, loneliness comes from not understanding and accepting the self. And I can gratefully say I have accepted myself.

Working with Aya

Before the retreat, we were introduced to the most important point: working with Aya is a conversation. It's like working with a doctor. If we go to a doctor and say tell me how to improve my life, the doctor might be quite generic. It can work, and we might feel better, yet when we ask something specific, like when we say: "My knee is hurting", they will know where to start and take it from there. The core symptoms might be a knee problem, but the cause is likely something else. The doctor's job is to figure out the cause and support us in healing it.

Working with Aya is similar; the more specific questions we have, the easier it will be for her to take us to the cause of the wound and support us in healing it. We can have different ways of asking. "Show me", "Help me" or "Teach me", then we add either an emotion (there are 6 main emotions - fear, anger, sadness, guilt, shame, joy) or an essential quality (love, trust, compassion, peace).

Since I learned about this, there have been two very present questions for me before the retreat started.

> **Please show me my fear.**
> **Please teach me how to trust.**

When I was contemplating my first question - the answer came to me:

> **"Your fear is your light, not your darkness."**

I have heard and read this before, in Course of Miracles, and Return to Love, written by Marianne Williamson:

> "Our deepest fear is not that we are inadequate. Our deepest fear is that we are powerful beyond measure. It is our light, not our darkness, that most frightens us. We ask ourselves, who am I to be brilliant, gorgeous, talented and fabulous? Actually, who are you not to be? You are a child of God[1]. Your playing small does not serve the world. There's nothing enlightened about shrinking so that other people won't feel insecure around you. We were born to manifest the glory of God that is within us. It's not just in some of us; it's in everyone." - Marianne Williamson

I've read and heard this before, yet, this time, this time it hit me deeper. This time it felt transformational. Not only

"Ah, ok I understand", but more "Ok, well, let me live like this then".

So I told myself - what if, what if I started living like this, in every area of my life? I am someone who sees challenges in any area of my life as opportunities for growth.

[1](you can replace the word God with spirit/universe/life essence)

As everything is 'figureoutable'. How can I make this situation work? How can I adapt and see the beauty in the rain? It's a gift and a curse, because I can talk myself into anything. Living in a small flat with lovely neighbours who are not very inspiring:

"Well, maybe I am here to inspire them; they're teaching me to stay grounded and peaceful.."

Living in cold rainy UK winters:

"Well, let me get more layers on. I will go for cold swims in winter; it's healthy. It all makes me appreciate the summer more."

And I could go on and on; I could be homeless and tell you, well, life is showing me I can handle this too, so I'll prove it that I can.

Well, I ask myself:

"What if the lesson from now on is to receive the abundance there is when I fully show up for life authentically, with grace and compassion? When I'm willing to face my "dramas" and transform them?".

There I had an immediate realisation, that I acted upon before heading to the group pick-up point for the retreat:

I am changing the Airbnb I'm staying after the retreat for a quieter place - an eco-lodge on the river, just outside Iquitos. I was worried about whether they'd be able to cook for me, with all the post-Aya-dieta requirements. However, I trust we'll figure it out. I will 'lose' some money as there is only a partial refund, but I don't see it as a loss.

Well, now let's see what Aya says about all of this!

Our deepest fear is not that we are inadequate, our deepest fear is that we are powerful beyond measure.

PART 2.
My Time At The Retreat

I am sitting literally on the river Moman in an eco-lodge in Iquitos. I see the edge of the jungle and while the boats pass by with all kinds of engine sounds, the owners' kids jump playfully into the water; I'm contemplating how to write this.

We 'got out' of the retreat yesterday, and I feel it's still a little hard to find words from time to time; they come and go. As if every cell of my body needs to catch up with all that just happened and let it land. Just like after a new system upgrade on my computer, a restart is needed, which takes a while, most of the time longer than the routine one.

That's the best way to describe where I'm at right now - restarting after an upgrade - while I do so, let me tell you what happened during these last 12 days that felt like many lifetimes.

Day 1

Our group was picked up from a hotel and driven by bus to a port. From there, we took 2 boats and headed to the jungle. The ride was serene; the huge river quickly turned into a narrow stream between trees, where my mind's main concern was - whether a monkey would jump on me, or I'd see a snake. Luckily, neither of them happened, and I could tune into my soul. And my soul was at peace, content, feeling like I'd experienced this before, in my dream or during some other lifetime.

Upon our arrival, sweet people from the village and The Temple were waiting for us with bottled water, walking sticks and umbrellas, ready to carry our bags so we could embark on the last part of our journey - a 30-minute walk through the jungle.
Just before we made a move, jungle rain started pouring down, and I proudly didn't take an umbrella - wanting to 'feel it all'. Luckily, the rain stopped after a while, and at the end of the walk, I couldn't tell if it was my sweat or the rain residues that were on me.

We were greeted by four facilitators, three of their assistants, a cute temple dog, and a nice fresh glass of camu camu* juice. After briefly explaining the area, the program for the rest of the day, and the rules - of which the most important one was the no use of mobile phones, we were guided into our tambos*. These little jungle huts had nets instead of actual windows and doors and consisted of a bed, hammock, toilet, sink, a few shelves and, importantly, an oil lamp. The showers were shared and there was no electricity in the temple area, except the kitchen and the laundry room.

My tambo was number 18 - at the very end of a little hill -

"Well, this will be a fun walk after a plant medicine ceremony",

I thought, but shortly after realising I was rewarded with a double tambo, I let any inner doubts go.

"This is awesome, more space, in the quietest corner of the area!"

- as if the universe knew my deepest needs.

After a delicious Aya-friendly lunch, we were given our first plant baths. In my head, and later discovering not only in mine, a plant bath would be a dip into something like a huge barrel filled with colourful flowers and essential oils. Just like you see on Instagram of all the wellness spa accounts. Candles, incense, ah, how divine...

Well, this was not quite it. A Peruvian jungle plant bath was something a little different... Two ladies, the herbalists, were standing in front of two huge buckets of water. You'd see and smell very small bits of herbs and flowers in these buckets. There was a little wooden stool in front of each bucket, and each of the ladies was holding

37

a smaller bucket, which she used to pour this mixture on the person sitting on the stool. From the head to the bottom, into the front of the swim pants and back of the swim pants. We were specifically asked to loosen the swimming gear in these areas for a short moment, to be cleansed properly.

Some got lucky and got more of the herbal mixture than others. The fun part of this was also the fact that we needed to let our bodies air-dry, not wash off any goodness. On my first day, I was one of the lucky ones, and I felt like a tea bag was poured over me. To be honest, my feelings were mixed; part of me really loved it, and part of me thought:

"How will I get this out of my hair and all other parts of my body?"

Well, considering this will happen every day now, I thought, Vanessa, the only thing you can do is surrender to this. You are in the jungle, and your hair and butt are filled with herbs; let's get this party started.

We spent the rest of the afternoon introducing ourselves and our intentions in a beautiful space called maloca*. A rounded wooden structure with palm leaf rooftop, wooden floors, huge mosquito net 'windows' and a very grounded feeling. This was the space where all the group sessions and Aya ceremonies were held.

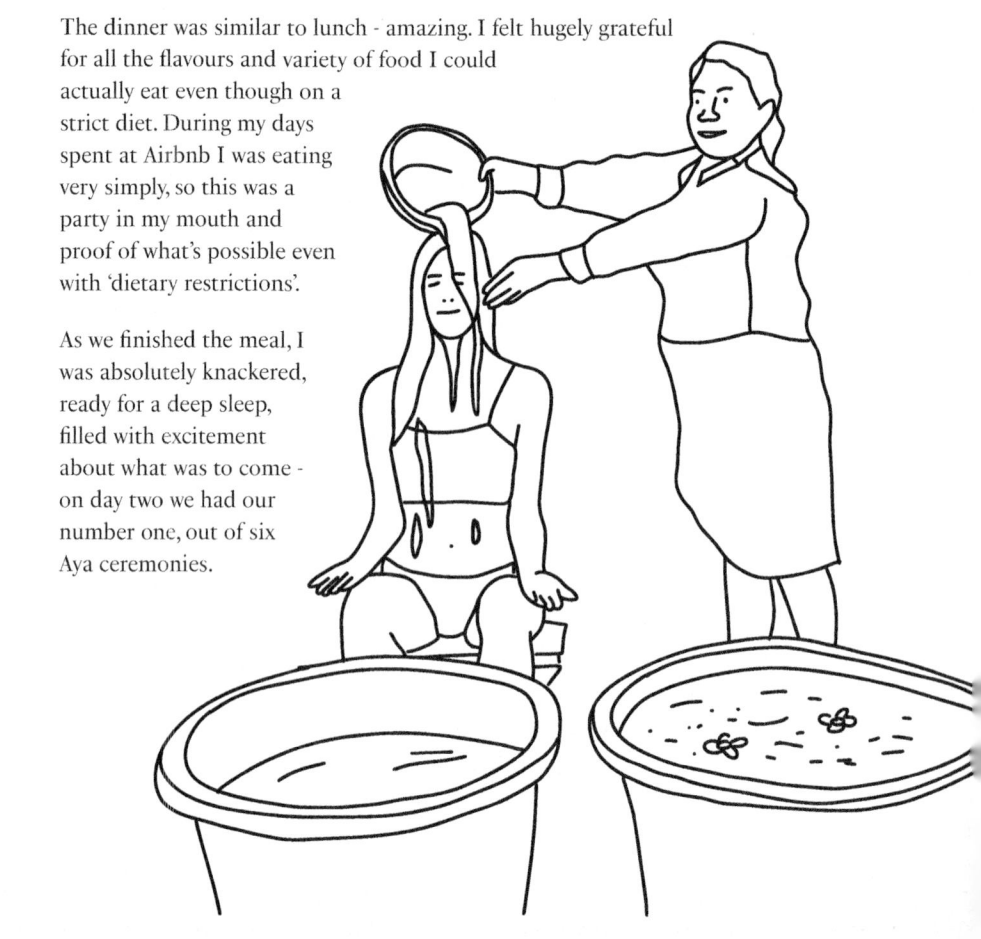

The dinner was similar to lunch - amazing. I felt hugely grateful for all the flavours and variety of food I could actually eat even though on a strict diet. During my days spent at Airbnb I was eating very simply, so this was a party in my mouth and proof of what's possible even with 'dietary restrictions'.

As we finished the meal, I was absolutely knackered, ready for a deep sleep, filled with excitement about what was to come - on day two we had our number one, out of six Aya ceremonies.

Day 2

First vapour bath

At 7.30am, we were in a queue for our first vapour baths. The best way to describe a jungle vapour bath is a single-steam sauna. The assistants brought a pot of boiling water with a lot of herbs, leaves, and flowers in front of a wooden chair. This chair was for one person to sit on; once the receiver got into their seated position, they were covered with this tent-like construction. It seemed as if we were sitting in a booth with a hot pot of herbs. The receiver was also given a stick to stir this beauty pot, to let the heat out and enjoy the steam and smell that it evaporates.

I went in with full confidence, stirring and stirring, thinking I didn't feel anything... until I did feel pretty much everything. I got really hot, really uncomfortable and went into claustrophobic panic:

"How am I gonna get out of here?", "I can't breathe", "I must get out", "I won't be able to last here for 10 minutes, no way."

My very old trauma was triggered. I am not sure where this comes from, but I have been very uncomfortable in closed spaces since I was a child. It's something I had been working on, and I thought I had healed this, as during the summer, I attended Sweatlodge[1], and I was fine.

Well, it was not quite healed yet, I guess. Surprised by my own reaction, I calmed myself down with deep, slow breaths. Telling myself:

"I am ok, there is enough space and air around me" I was able to last the 10 minutes and survive. Getting out, I was still surprised about what just happened, and needed to sit and contemplate this for a while. I told myself:

"Well, what a great place to be, to heal this now and forever."

After a yummy brekkie, a full-on day of 'induction' started:

We met the Shipibo* healers all sitting next to each other in the circle with us. The maestros*, the curanderos*, as they're called, Toni, Jorge, Edith, and Laura, were the main healers who were going to be in the ceremonies with us and transmit the actual healing. Inocencia - the herbalist, her assistant whose name I just can't remember and Cintia - their cook. None of them spoke English, a couple of them Spanish, and all of them their Shipibo language. It took them between 14 hours to 30 hours to get to The Temple from their villages, and they will be staying with us in their casa on The Temple grounds throughout the retreat.

[1] A ceremony practiced by various indigenous cultures for purification and spiritual renewal through sweating rituals involving heated rocks, water and darkness.

The way the ceremonies work is that the healers and space holders sit in the middle of the maloca on mattresses, while all of the attendees have their mattresses in the circle around them. When the healers feel the group is ready, they note one of the space holders. The medicine is then served. The attendees walk up to the centre, one by one, sit down, connect to their intention and receive a glass of Aya to drink.

While one of the curandero, in our case always Edith, pours the glass, one facilitator asks how we are feeling, and the other offers to take a mapacho* to our mattress spot with us.

The mapacho is to be puffed or just held in our hand from time to time throughout the ceremony, in order to help us with grounding and connecting to our initial intention. Once everyone receives their Aya serving, the oil lamps are switched off, and we wait in complete darkness, sitting or lying on our mattresses.

Again, once the healers feel the space is ready, they start singing as a group a type of song called ikaro*, the medicine song of the Shipibo tribe. Then they each go and sit in front of one person and start singing to them. The ikaro is specifically sung to the one person the healer sits in front of. So, each ikaro is unique and its words depend on the receiver's energy, pains, fears, and support needed. However, all four of the ikaros have a similar melody, so it's not distracting for the ones that are around.

The receiver should sit up with open arms during the receiving of the ikaro - to show commitment and presence and to feel the ikaro in the most powerful way. Each ikaro is about 8 minutes long, after which the healer blesses the receiver with Aqua de Florida*, and moves to the next person. By the end of the ceremony, each attendee receives four ikaro healings, in our case, sung by two male and two female maestros.

The peak time and effect of Aya is felt by each person differently, of course, and it supports the healing power of the Ikaro. Apparently, a long time ago, it was the healer who drank the Aya; the receiver would 'only' receive the Ikaro, without drinking the medicine. As one of the facilitators said -

"You would probably have to be really troubled if you wanted to come all the way to the jungle to listen to a song. So yes, we serve the medicine as well. This helps you connect more to what you're healing while the healing is happening."

The medicine and the healing trigger a variety of purges* - the most common are vomiting, diarrhoea, sweating, feeling very cold, shaking or short numbness of different body parts, crying and need for movement. The receiver, very often, sees different visions, which come in the form of patterns or actually full stories, just like a dream does. These are not necessary for the 'healing to work'. Some people see more than others, some purge more than others, and some people sense more than others. It truly varies from person to person, and healing to healing. The Ikaro and Aya are doing what they need to be, always.

We were told the first ceremony would be a gentle one; it would be an introduction to the medicine, something like a greeting. I was really excited, curious, grateful, and, to be honest, to my surprise, quite fearless. I knew this was where I was meant to be, whatever happens, happens. I could feel my intention of trusting myself and the spirit was truly coming to life. However, I did have one worry -

"What if I need to go to the toilet and can't walk properly?"

The team had this one covered, as the way we would call facilitators if we needed anything during the ceremony was to use our head torch in the red light setting and point it at the wall our mattress was in front of. Someone would then come and ask what we need. There would also be a couple of so-called 'door angels' - two sweet men standing next to the entrance, pointing their red light (as the white light was just too bright in the darkness) at the stairs and at the available toilet if someone needed to go. So, in theory, this was all covered, but the mind does what the mind does sometimes, and mine was thinking about this toilet issue a lot.

Our group consisted of 23 people coming from different areas of the world: the US, England, Japan, Europe, and Australia. Each one of us came with a range of life stories, intentions, and experiences with healing; most of us have never worked with Aya, and you would be able to tell there was loads of fear and curiosity in the group.

After a day filled with information, I was shattered. I was ready to go to bed and sleep it off, however the ceremony was waiting and some preparation was needed. Our last meal during ceremony days was lunch, there was no food allowed after 2 pm and no liquid after 5pm.

At 5, we got our plant baths and were asked to be in the maloca all ready for 6.30pm. This meant bringing our head torches, blankets, layers of clothes, a Florida water essence, which we received, and any small things we would like to bring as 'energy support'.

We had an hour of yin yoga before each ceremony to relax us and get us out of our heads. Well, I was so out of my head at some point that I took a power nap during the yoga session.

The space looked magical, with only a few oil lamps lit up, the full moon shining outside, and everyone sitting around in the circle on their mattresses waiting for the healers to arrive (further on I'll call them mats for the ease and beauty of it, however, these were actually very thick and soft). I felt in and out between being amazed at how beautiful it all looked and how tired I was.

The ceremony had finally started and I got to walk for my first 'shot' of Aya. We were recommended to drink it in one go, as the taste was apparently not very pleasant. I kneeled on the cushion in front of the serving trio. When one of the facilitators asked me:

"How are you feeling today?"

All I could say was, "Good." I mean, really, I was good; I was ready and in full anticipation of what was coming next. Edith, one of the healers, then handed me the glass which she poured the medicine into. A small portion, about 1/3 of a shot glass. As I took it in before I drank, I blessed the glass with my intention:

"Please show me how to trust myself."

I must admit, I actually liked the taste. The medicine tasted like a grapefruit smoothie to me. Then it was time to walk back to my spot, be patient, as thoughtless as possible, not fall asleep and let the medicine and healers do 'their work.'

After about 15 minutes, as the healers sang the group ikaro, I had this beautiful vision of a forest. Lots of different species of plants moved around and talked to each other. I really wanted to sing and dance, but this was not the space for it, so I just sang a bit of gibberish (nonsense from the unconscious brain) very quietly to myself and moved around while sitting.

I got tired quite quickly, and my back started hurting from all the sitting. Therefore, I really wanted to lie down. Slightly worried that I'll fall asleep, I did give myself permission to put my head on the mat and cover my body with a warm blanket, surrendering to it all, telling myself I just won't sleep. I managed to rest and then sit up for my first ikaro, which was from Toni, about 15 minutes after the group one.

My body was getting tingly, and I could feel my solar plexus warming up, then my lower abdomen, my legs and lastly, my hands, all in a very comfortable way. I felt like the medicine was going through every cell of my body and greeting me. I was honestly fascinated,

"Wow, this is it... So it's happening, I wonder what will happen next."

In all honesty, not much happened next, apart from me being really tired, switching between sitting and lying; I saw a few bright colours and glimpses of different places in nature, such as waterfalls or forests. It was really hard to get into the visions more. I wanted to go on a journey and discover these places, but I kept coming out into the 3D world - the space around me, checking when the next healer was coming, so I was ready to sit up. I had a few attempts at trying to light up the mapacho. The tricky bit with this one was that we needed to cover the lighter as the fire light would distract the healers. So imagine a non-smoker, sitting half asleep in complete darkness, holding this natural cigarette in her mouth while trying to light it without inhaling the actual smoke. Yes, I stayed with my attempts, thinking I will rather practise this the next day.

Despite not drinking 3 hours before the ceremony, my need for pee was very high, I could swear I had not drunk an equal amount of water to what was going out. It's as if all the unnecessary liquids in my body were coming out. I actually never asked if peeing this often could be one of the ways of purging, I would say yes, as number 2 certainly was.

All that said, basically, I was a bit unsettled; luckily always able to sit and receive the beautiful ikaros from each healer. I think I did fall asleep after my last one; as I just remember the words of one of the facilitators:

"And the ceremony is now closed." While saying "Gracias" and "Buenas noches",

the healers walked out of the maloca, and a beautiful silence and calmness were felt all around.

In a few minutes, some of us started packing up our ceremony gear and decided to walk back to our tambos, while others stayed in the maloca. To keep the energy peaceful and let everyone be in their space, all needed to be done in complete silence and darkness or using only the red light of our head torches.

I had decided I would like the comfort of my bed and the space of my tambo, so I walked back. To my surprise, I found my tambo without getting lost in the curvy paths or stepping on any creatures. And that was ceremony one done; I fell asleep like a very happy baby, making sure my alarm was on, as at 7.30 am, we had to be showered and ready to queue for our vapour baths.

Apparently, it's great to let Aya do its work overnight. However, it's highly recommended to shower in the morning thereafter, wash off all those purges we had consciously or subconsciously realised overnight and reconnect to the body and the present 3D reality.

Day 3

I must say, I was a little bit concerned about these vapour baths, keeping in mind my previous experience. As always, trying to see the glass half full, my inner voice was telling me:

"Well, now I know what's coming, I'm ready for it, it will be fine."

It was semi-fine. I didn't feel very comfortable, and I definitely needed to focus on my breathing and being in my body a lot rather than the space with the heat all around me. It was not a smooth pampering 10 minutes, that's for sure. I was happy to be out, taking some time to be with the emotions that had arisen and let them pass.

To be honest, I was slightly annoyed that people who were in the queue, waiting for their turn to get into the vapour booth, were chatting a lot. My mind was going,

"You really don't feel this? It's such a deep experience for those who are in the booth. Can you not hold the space properly? And be silent."

However, we don't know what we don't know, and unless I shared this view with them, they probably would have no idea, as their experience seemed to be very different from mine.

Considering sharing this view with the facilitators, I asked myself:

"What's my lesson in this? Is it sharing my concerns with others? Asking for more silence? Or can I see this as a practice of being fully connected to my breath and body, regardless of what others are doing?"

Knowing there would be only one more vapour bath, I decided to see it as a practice of 'staying in my lane' while the 'world around is a mess.'

"And I can always ask 'Doctor Aya' when I am working with her next time." I thought.

Until early afternoon we had individual physical consultations with the healers. This meant each one of us had a dedicated time slot for a chat while the rest had free time for introspection and relaxation time. I spent most of my time sleeping, journaling, and connecting to what happened in the previous ceremony and what I would like to work with, in the following ceremony.

As I entered the maloca to have my physical consultation with the healers, I felt overwhelmed. In my mind, this would see one healer and one, maybe two facilitators. Ha ha, haven't I learned yet, not to have expectations?

This was the whole committee; everyone, including the course assistants, was sitting in a half circle, across which was a chair for me to sit on. It was really intimidating and uncomfortable. I find physical health hugely important. At a health coaching course I had done in the past, we were asked to read the book 'Your Body Never Lies' and I couldn't express it better than this title. Our body knows before we know, it's the best guide and I always try to listen. Sometimes, I don't act upon what it says until I really really have to, yet to give myself a good tap on the shoulder, this has improved a lot in the past years.

I wasn't sure what to share, as gratefully, there was nothing major with my physical body, apart from the occasional back pain that goes when I stop working and sitting behind the computer all day. There are things from the past that reoccur when I'm not in touch with my body, such as low iron. Or things that I just won't be able to heal - such as my eyesight. Or things that I am very aware of, such as feeling bloated after eating, when I don't pay attention to the food but to my thoughts or to conversation with someone else. I know this; it's something I'm constantly working on and need to be aware of, rather than something that will be healed by taking any natural or unnatural medicine.

As I thought, I am entering this new way of being - allowing myself to receive; I shared most of these 'issues', thinking maybe there'll be something I don't know, a different view, or some yummy natural juices I won't harm taking anyway. After leaving, I did feel like a hypochondriac, like I was digging into something that really didn't need any more digging. I think sometimes our mind makes things much more dramatic than they are. Of course, there is a balance, and no concern should be left unattended if we feel there is an issue. I didn't, hence I felt a little weird about the whole thing.

However, I was happy to know we'll be receiving plant remedies the following afternoon and every morning thereafter to replace my not-so-favourite vapour bath. Drinking ginger juice with honey and some other goodnesses and having a massage every other morning, I was most certainly not afraid of.

The afternoon ended with a beautiful, peaceful yoga session guided by one of the extended members of the facilitator's team. I had stopped yoga for a while as my osteopath suggested it was not the best for my back, and I had been focusing on my quantum flow practice, running, and swimming. I realised how much I missed the slow breath, stretching and feeling fully in my body with a gentle practice. There and then, I made an intention to reconnect with my yoga flow at least a couple of times a week. I was still experiencing a lot of tiredness.

I hadn't felt this tired for a long time, and from the outside perspective, I was really not doing much. Yet internally, this journey was a huge shift, so I allowed myself to listen to my body and, after dinner, go for a deep 12-hour sleep.

Let's step out of my retreat experience for a moment

Now it's probably the best time to share a bit about my spiritual connection. Since I was very little, since I can remember my thoughts really, I have had an internal dialogue. This voice that I am in conversations with, pretty much all the time. Recently, I have learned that not everyone has this. Apparently, some people think in spoken sentences, and others don't. They just visualise, feel or know and 'translate' this knowing into an actual conversation. However, they don't have this constant internal voice. How amazing is it to see how beautifully different we are?

Recently, I have started noticing and being able to differentiate very clearly, when this inner dialogue is with my ego and when it is with my soul. Very simply put, the conversations with the ego are tough, indecisive, noisy and filled with doubt, self-sabotage, judgement and fear. The conversations with the soul are empowering, loving, graceful, and filled with confidence, honesty and guidance.

From this place, from the dialogue with the soul's voice, I can connect to seeing things rather than just having an internal dialogue. Usually with the support of sound, drum beat, or very conscious breathing, when I close my eyes, I truly get to go on a journey. Like in a dream, but I'm not asleep, a whole story is created for me that I see and have conversations with animals, people or plants. I can just ask a question, and I receive an answer; sometimes, the answer is not quick, and I don't see or hear it right away. Sometimes I'm asked to wait for the answer and listen for it in my everyday life. Sometimes, the answer comes through a conversation with a friend, not necessarily because of exactly what they say. It's more like reading or feeling between the lines of what they say. Sometimes, the answer comes in the form of a book, a song, or a 'random' post I read. It's an inner knowing that now I have received my answer.

From a spiritual perspective, these people or animals are called 'Spirit Guides', I like to describe them as 'The Highest Self'. They come in the form of a person or animal, yet it's still us, guiding us, just the purest version of us, that's connected to all there is. It's not a random tiger that's telling me which fund to invest my money into, or where to move. It's still me, talking to me, yet in a version that I don't connect to constantly. And sometimes it's easier to hear the answer when it's personified.

I used to ignore this 'soul insert dialogue' or not give it much meaning, judging it. The ego-inner dialogue was winning over the soul one. And I do still question it sometimes.
Is this my subconscious mind? Is this my imagination? Is this my intuition? God? The spirit? I understand the science of the subconscious mind a little. However, I'm not the best person to share this knowledge because I often forget the facts a few moments after I read them. I've gotten to the point where I personally don't need to understand every detail of this. I go with it and see what happens. Does it matter if I call it intuition, imagination, or divine guidance? To me, right now, it doesn't. What matters is that it works, that I feel better, and that the decisions I make from this place are making me happy, making me feel alive, inspiring others to feel the same, and are aligning with the highest good for all.

So, a lot of my introspections throughout the days of working with Aya came from this place. They became a dialogue between me and the medicine. So me and the highest version of me. I asked and I received an answer. Not always the one I would expect, not always the one that was easy to take in, always one that was necessary. Some were related to my life, to people who are in it, to my work; others to the very present moment and the ceremonies. Some of this dialogue is meant to be shared in this book, some with specific people, some throughout the months and years to come and some is meant to stay between me and Me.

Day 4

The day started slow, which meant more time for sleep, writing, internal dialogue with myself and conversations with the sweet souls from the group. All the people from the group have been lovely, very kind and easy to chat with. However, for me, the chats have been distracting sometimes. Well, let's reframe it: they were testing me on how much I can stay in my own lane and not get carried away by the sharings and opinions of others, while staying open to hearing them and changing mine if I feel it's appropriate.

Yet, during this kind of internal work and healing, I quickly realised how much quiet and 'me time' I needed, and I had a word with myself not to feel any fear of missing out, or guilt, just because I don't involve myself in socialising very often.

We had a group meeting in the afternoon, to learn more about what type of plant remedies we'll be taking and the process of receiving them. As well as a short preparation to connect with our intention for ceremony number two. From this time onwards, we would get more of the Aya medicine to start with, and we could ask for a second serving, in the timeframe between our 1st and 3rd ikaro.

Same as the first, and all the further ones, the ceremony started at 8 pm, following a yin yoga session. My intention was:

> "Please show me how to heal my fear."

As I had still felt quite uncomfortable in the morning vapour baths, I really would have liked to heal this one.

It was during the group ikaro, when I was lying on my mat with my eyes closed, simply waiting for what would happen, when I found myself being under the earth. Deep down in the soil. You know, as you can see in some books, the cut-through of the earth and ants walking in one of these ant tunnels. I was in one, thinking of my intention, how I would like to heal this fear of closed places and not having enough air to breathe. I heard a very clear voice:

> "Just look around, you're under the earth, in a closed tunnel, and you are absolutely fine, breathing perfectly."

I had to laugh out loud, telling myself,

> "Yes, yes, I AM absolutely fine."

Then, this wonderful world opened up, filled with bright, clear blue skies and flowers in all shapes and forms. I was wowed.

> "When you feel you don't have space, just create it energetically, close your eyes, breathe and create all the space you need around you and you'll be absolutely fine."

> "We are the creators of our reality, of the space around us. No matter how small or uncomfortable the space might seem from the outside, it's our vibration that matters. It's our vibration that can shift even the most bleak and dark space into wonderland. It's light that enlightens the dark."

I was still really tired; I felt like I was done while the ceremony had only started. My mind was thinking:

"How long will this whole thing take?",
"Should I go and get more?",
"I think I'll be ok to get more.",
"When do I need to sit up again?",
"Just don't fall asleep.",
"Should I be throwing up?",
"Why is that person making so many sounds?",
"I wonder what he is feeling like.",
"Vanessa focus, focus and don't fall asleep.",
"But what do I focus on?".

Maestro Toni finally came to sit in front of me, and I was receiving my first ikaro. I felt very empowered, tall, and grounded. I heard a very kind, yet confident and determined voice speaking to me:

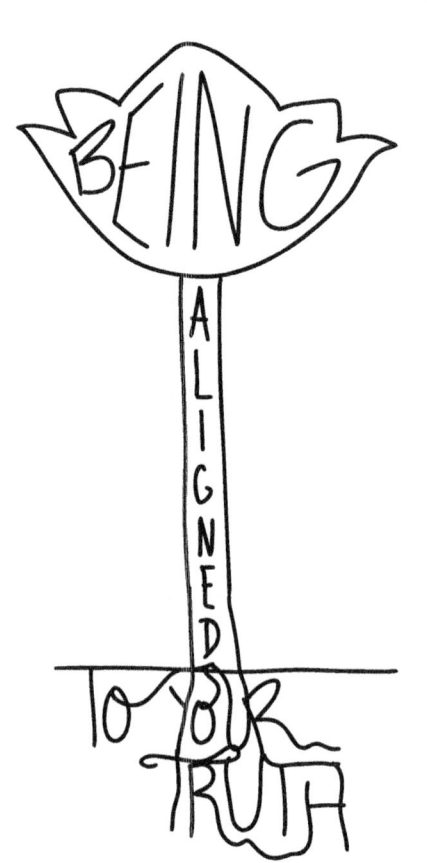

"Look, this, your life, it's your work. I am not going to do this for you. I can not live and sort out your life for you. However, I can, and will, show you how to stay focused and fully connected to yourself without being affected by others' thoughts or actions. Then it's your practice and you'll need to practise it often. You'll get stronger and more energised, and with time, your practice will become easier. I'll always be here, to remind you of this, in case you forget. Anytime you feel your energy is dispersed, take a deep breath, squeeze your body and imagine you're the stem of a flower. A thick stem, whose juice is your essence, your breath. You're rooted deep down in the earth, having long, deep roots. Your flower blooms at the top of your head or your eyes or your heart. Wherever you want your flower to be at that moment, that's the place you'll be open to the world. The rest you keep protected in your stem. Zip the air in and breathe."

I got it; I could really embody being the stem of a flower for a moment and feel rooted within my body.

> "Ok, ok, great, thank you! This is my practice, from now on."

Feeling a lot of excitement with a sprinkle of disappointment -

> "Can you not help me even a little bit? Is it all really all up to me only?".

> "Well, it's really up to you only, to be in your body. It's also up to you to allow yourself support and to choose people around you who make you feel in your body without effort. You'll know who these are. It's up to you to live in places that make you feel truly you; it's up to you to choose professions that help you stay within. It's all here for you, so you really don't need to do it alone. You have as much help as you'd like if you choose so."

After the ikaro finished, I stayed with my lesson for a moment and decided it was time to get more medicine and see what happened next. I lit up my red light and pointed it at the maloca wall behind me. In only a few seconds later, an assistant came to me, asking what I needed. He gently helped me get up and walked with me to the centre, where I was served a second glass of Aya.

Receiving the next ikaro from Jorge felt like a dance with a rainbow. It was beautiful, fun, sensual and loving. My mind was trying to figure it out:

> "What is this?,
> Who am I dancing with?,
> Why are there two rainbows?"

The moment I got hung up on these thoughts, the dance vanished, and I couldn't see anything. The answer was simple:

> "Just surrender, let it happen at its own timing and don't try to figure it all out. You'll know exactly what this means when you're ready to know; meanwhile, enjoy this bliss and try not to push it away with your thoughts. And remember, you can connect to this vibration anytime you decide to do so."

My third ikaro was from Edith. What I saw was amazingly visual; I mean all of those journeys were, yet this one was so much more colourful and 3D. The area just above and between my eyebrows, my third eye, opened up. I literally saw this massive purple and pink eye coming out of my forehead while loads of different patterns, colours, and flowers started coming out of it. I was in and out of this 'colourful reality.' Getting lost in these mesmerising patterns and colours, like going down a fantastic rabbit hole, while trying not to fall asleep in this seated position and honour the healing and healer.

My last ikaro from Laura felt really nourishing. It felt like I was being pampered by the earth. I found myself in the middle of a warm forest, in a dark turquoise pond that was filled with pink, purple and white water lilies and lotuses. I was surrounded by butterflies, while sloths, monkeys and snakes were all around in the jungle.

> **"Whenever you need to recharge, this is your place. Come here often. This place is filled with all the medicine, the minerals, and the care your body needs at that moment. No need to fear, just allow yourself to sit and let all the goodness in."**

Immediately after the ikaro finished, I laid down in this bliss and fell asleep. I woke up briefly, as the healers were leaving and saying their "Buenos Noches". After what seemed like an hour, however, I couldn't really tell; I woke up in this bliss and decided to go back to my tambo.

After settling into my comfy bed and being ready to ride the wave of this blissful state, a storm was about to start, and I noticed some weird sounds around. Lots and lots of wind, jungle noise and pouring rain. All of a sudden, my head decided to question all the noise, and I became really scared.

"Is it someone here?",
"Is someone trying to get into my tambo?",
"A jungle animal?",
"A creepy person?".

All the people in the retreat seemed very nice, but what if this medicine turned them into weirdos?

The sounds, in combination with the fact that I was quite open and vulnerable after the healing, triggered this deep and old trauma. Fortunately, I was able to not buy into it fully. I kept saying to myself:

"Don't be silly, this is just in your mind. You are absolutely fine and safe. It's just jungle noise. Breathe deeply and try to fall asleep."

After a while, I got up and checked the tambo area with my torch. Not to my surprise, I had seen nothing, so slightly more satisfied and calmer, I was able to close my eyes and fall asleep.

I did have a very unusual dream about befriending a snake - a huge anaconda. Normally, I am really scared of snakes; even seeing them in a photo gives me goosebumps, but in this dream, I was absolutely fine; I was stroking and patting the snake, talking to it, as if it was my best friend. Even waking up after, I didn't feel grossed out, I felt at complete peace. I think I was befriending all my fears, acknowledging that they're there, while not letting them run the show.

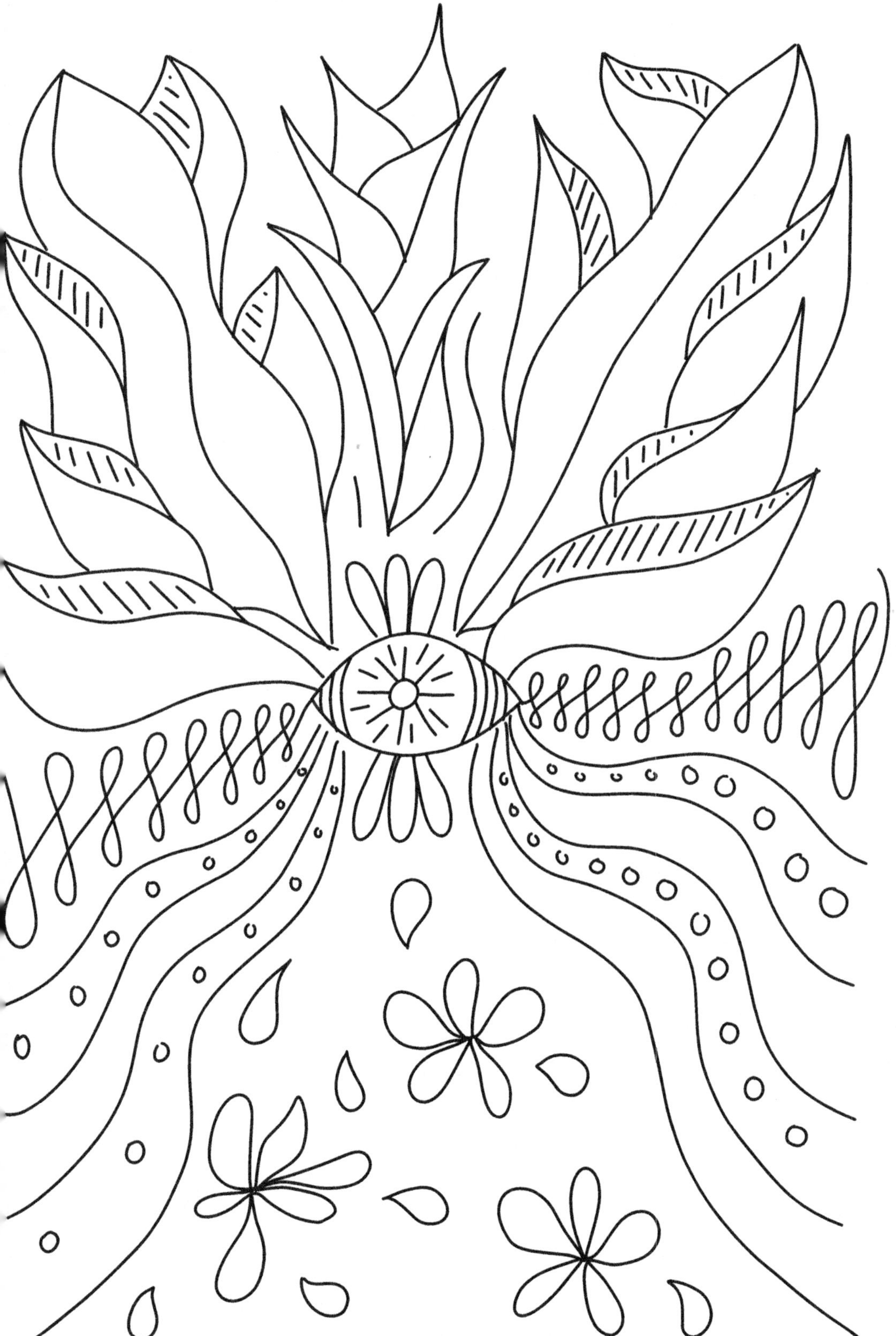

Day 5

This morning, we received our first plant remedies and massages. All of us were sat in an outdoor waiting area, and one by one, we walked up to a table to get a range of colourful drinks.

After this taste-bud adventure, some of us were sent into the healer's casa to get a massage. As divine as it was, throughout the following days, I learned to come at a later time and avoid waiting with the very friendly mosquito for too long.

My favourites were a glass of camu camu with honey - great for digestion and cleansing the blood; and a glass of ginger with honey - a warming immune system booster. Those two I kept to drink the last, as the ginger left me feeling warmed up and energised.

The rest of the drinks were great for calming, grounding, cleansing the liver and opening the heart. I was also given a mixture of these in my water bottle to be taken with me and drank during the day. A nice treat, that left me feeling like I was very cared for.

The massages were fantastic - short and effective. I was very grateful for receiving all of this; however, if I had any expectations for the retreat, it was that there would be even more emphasis on these remedies and on our body overall, throughout the whole time.

For some, this type of care-taking, using a few natural remedies, eating well and avoiding certain food groups - such as processed sugar or alcohol, was quite a new experience.
I have been practising eating well, and treating myself with natural remedies since I attended my holistic course. I can't really remember when was the last time I took an ibuprofen or any sort of Western meds. It was a great reminder to have no expectations, acknowledge all the care the herbalist put into preparing these, and give myself a tap on the shoulder for nourishing myself pretty well over the past years.

As the day progressed, I was still contemplating the fear from my previous night - it didn't fully leave me. I wondered what the best way to handle it was. My mind got in the way, and I questioned myself:

"Should've I gone deeper into the fear and seen what would happen rather than tried to stop it?"

For this one, I decided to have a conversation with one of the facilitators and asked what the ideal action to take in this situation would be. She basically said exactly what I had done and asked me:

"Imagine someone else was scared; what would you tell them?"

She also invited me to look at where this fear comes from and what trauma gets triggered. That I knew, and I knew it's also an ancestral and collective trauma, it's not only mine. The fear of being abused, in any form - emotionally, physically, sexually, is a collective fear of many women and men. And unfortunately, it's valid. We still live in a world where force, abuse and will to prove one's power over another, exists.

After my conversation with the facilitator, I realised there was one thing I had done, that wasn't in the highest alignment, in my opinion - I slightly dismissed the fear. I told myself

"Don't be silly",

before even checking the space. The truth is I could've been right, I didn't really know until I checked. Regardless of how ridiculous the thought of someone else being around my Tambo, in a safe space like this, might've seemed to me, saying "Don't be silly" to my scared self was not the ideal choice of words. This I have learned.

I am definitely not saying we should live in fear and paranoia, checking all the time if someone is following us. However, I think when the fear arises for some reason, it's important to treat it gently. As that intuition is likely pointing us to something, within us or outside us. And it's important not to dismiss it. In my case, it was showing me a greater awareness of self and the outside world.

The entire day was dedicated to relaxation and reflection, until ceremony number three in the evening. We were joking with some about how quickly and easily the day passes while being in a hammock. Yes, yes, it did, and I felt zero guilt about it. Every cell of the body basically needs to catch up with all of these upgrades and new ways of being. Honestly, all I had done was journal, take loads of naps, eat lunch, hold some short chats, and get ready for the whole 'thing' again. Plant baths, air drying, 'gear' packing, yin yoga, and then ceremony number three was on.

I hadn't felt this before the other ceremonies, but with this one, I was uncomfortable. Fidgety and not very excited about it, as I didn't want to feel the fear from last night again. However, I knew this might be part of it. Some people see things in ceremonies that are quite uncomfortable, that's when the purge comes in - to release the fears and move through them. Yet, I was still doubtful to do this. Telling myself:

"Whatever will be, will be. I'll ask the medicine to help me with this fear."

I walked up to the middle of the circle and was served a full glass of grandmother Aya.

After a short time, I noticed my annoyance - wondering if the medicine was working; as I hadn't seen or felt anything yet.

"It's been only a few minutes!!"

But still, my "I want" - my ego - was quite overpowering in this situation. I kept trying to connect to my intention, but the ego side of me was distracting me. I began to question everything - the space, the people, wondering why am I really here. Thankfully the group ikaro started and calmed this inner voice of mine, while my body began to shake a lot. I laid down on the mat, covered myself with a blanket and surrendered to it completely. I was shaking off this whole 'mind drama' as I saw this red energy, something that looked like a long red scarf, leaving my body.

As maestro Toni came to sit in front of me and began to sing, I was annoyed again; I was fighting this whole process with my mind, telling myself, that I didn't understand why I needed to sit when I want to lie down, I was basically in a massive tantrum with the present moment. Right up until I started seeing this blurry dot of something, coming right up to me. I wasn't scared; I was intrigued; I was safe and focused as this dot turned into a beautiful jaguar, peacefully walking towards me. I began to feel his wise presence, and a deep conversation about fears was initiated. We talked about my fears of being a woman, my fears of being in the dark, my fears of being attacked by something and my fears of being manipulated by someone.

"The simplest way of feeling safe is to call upon light; it's not naive, it's not weak, it's the greatest thing you can do for yourself and anyone else. The darkness is afraid of the light, more than the light is of the darkness, remember this."

"The light isn't only a soft and fluffy fairy; look at me. I'm a jaguar, and I'm the light, too! Its pure intentions are what differentiate the darkness from light, not the size, colour, gender or texture. The darkness can be disguised under a 'pretty fluffy mask', yet from now on, you'll know. And whenever you're unsure, whenever you don't know whom to trust, or whenever you feel fear, just call upon me, and I'll show you what to do."

As our conversation finished, it was as if someone zoomed out of this close-up visual and saw a scene of the two of us walking side by side, on the top of a mountain at dusk.

I started getting myself together, feeling much less agitated, more present, and feeling the importance of being here, for this retreat and on the earth for a reason.

> **"Life will be tough sometimes, you'll feel fears, that's inevitable. Remember, you're the light, when you live as such, you'll always be safe. You create your safety, you surround yourself with safety, and you'll know how to treat the darkness with your presence.**
> **The more you think about the possibility of fear, the harder life will be. The more you believe in the power of your own light, the more peaceful your life will be. Light attracts light and creates more light."**

As Jorge arrived to sing the ikaro for me, I sat up and felt a lot of sharp pain in my solar plexus. I did my best to stay focused on the song rather than the pain and the mind wanderings, going into what it is all about.

Suddenly, I found myself holding a stem with a small fluffy bud at the top of it. First, I didn't know what I was meant to do with this one; I kept looking at it and twisting the stem in my hands while holding it in front of me. Still feeling lots of pain in the middle of my body, I began to breathe into it more deeply, expanding and contracting my solar plexus, while still holding this random thing in my hands. As I was with it, this fluffy bud started becoming bigger and brighter. With every deep breath I took, the circle in front of me would expand into more light. Just like a lamp starting to shine brighter, expanding all around me. I found myself in this bubble of light, and my pain stopped. Not just a little, it completely stopped. I felt like 'I am back'; the annoyance was gone, the body shaking was gone; the wonders and wanders of my mind were gone, and my decision about getting a second glass of Aya was clear:

"I am not getting another serving; I'll let this be, what it is. I'm fully satisfied and I don't need more."

The next two ikaros were filled with joy, love and nourishment. Dancing around in nature, by the sea, first on my own, then with family and a loving community of people. All of us dancing around the fire on the beach. There was no sense of who any of these people were; I didn't recognise them, and I didn't need to know; the essence was what mattered. The vibration that it made me feel was the golden gem of those journeys. There was a lot of motherly love, care and a feeling of safety within while sharing myself with others.

I stayed in the maloca for a while after the ceremony had ended and the healers left, enjoying this joyful vision. Later on, as I decided to make my way to my tambo, I walked in complete peace and fell asleep without any fear, as if I were on a fluffy cloud.

Day 6

This was the day of reflections and integrations - first on our own, and later on, all of us together in a group session.

As I was journaling and reflecting on the previous ceremonies, I really noticed and appreciated one fundamental fact - the balance between masculine and feminine healers in the ceremony.

I had been receiving the first two ikaros from male and the second two from female healers and I could easily feel the difference. They each brought up different strengths in a different way.

The masculine energy was direct, caring, empowering and strict; they brought up the "You've got this, and you have to stay committed to it", "You're protected, as long as you keep doing 'the work'."

The feminine were nourishing, gentle, soft, graceful, joyful and calm. They brought up the "Play" "Dance" "Envision", "Create" "Share Yourself."

Both were equally unconditionally loving and dedicated.

The balance between the feminine and masculine is one of the most important dances we can all do for this earth. Within ourselves and in relation to one another. I have never been 'against men' or 'pro women'. There isn't one better than another, neither do I think that women should act like men and visa versa. Of course, there are fundamental rights we all have to have the same. However, we are different, too. Men's inner circles work in a 24-hour rhythm, while women's in a 28-day one. Our peak performance time is different, what our bodies need to eat at certain times is different, and the way we create projects and take on challenges is different. And that is wonderful. We are meant to empower these strengths within each other, rather than try to embody what's not really meant for us. The more self-aware and balanced we are within, the easier this becomes to implement in relation to the other.

"The healed feminine doesn't need to disempower the masculine in order to claim herself, and the healed masculine doesn't need to disempower the feminine in order to claim himself."

The healings transmitted through each of the maestros I have received so far were the ultimate proof of this.

It was also the last day of 2023, so before dinner, we got a bonus plant bath to clean all the unnecessary junk from the year. Why not? Anything that will help me welcome and embrace the new year, I'm all for.

Between a few of us, we made a semi-joke plan of starting to create The New Year Plant Bath Parties in cities we had lived, like London and NYC. For all the people who are looking for something other than drinking or partying.

How epic would this be? Imagine a rooftop terrace with heated lamps, filled with loads of colourful plants all around, serving fresh coconut bowls, fruity smoothies and big buckets of blessed plant water that can be poured on you to clear all the unnecessary energies from last year. I mean, I got pretty excited about this and even offered my shamanic drumming services. I got a little carried away here, but seriously if you're up for it, get in touch.

This New Year celebration, however, was spent in the cosiness of our own beds; I think I can speak for all of us - we were really happy to have a 'night off' and sleep off all the ceremony upgrades.

Day 7

This morning, after breakfast, we were supposed to go for a plant medicine walk. In our minds, this was an hourly long walk deep through the jungle; we were told to wear rain boots and protect ourselves with long sleeves and trousers because of all the mosquitoes and insects around us. Some of us even grabbed our walking sticks from the first walk to the temple.

As we arrived at our meet-up point, we saw the facilitators wearing flip-flops and most of the healers being barefoot; all of us laughed at the ridiculousness of the situation and how overdressed we were because, in the end, we truly walked just around the corner, 5 minutes outside of the Temple area. There we found the Ayahuasca vine, Chacruna plant and Caminuri tree. The three most important plants the maestros were dieting at some point in their lives as part of their apprenticeship and initiations to become healers and be able to share their gifts with others fully. They would diet these separately, with only specific types of foods throughout the length of 3 months to a year. This would allow them to connect deeply to the spirit of the plant, understand it and support them in providing healing to others.

In our ceremonies, the Ayahuasca brew has always been made with two plants - the Ayahuasca vine and the leaf of the Chacruna plant. Aya is the ingredient that makes our bodies purge and release the old patterns and stories - anything that stops us from being the highest version of ourselves. While Chacruna is the ingredient that gives us visions, however, the activation of the Chacruna plant is only possible in combination with the Aya vine. So essentially, taking either plant on their own, one wouldn't have had any visions. While there is scientific proof and explanation of why these two plants work together well, it's very unlikely the Shamnas thousands of years ago would have known about this. They believe it's the plants who originally told the Shamans how to create the ayahuasca brew.

If you're interested in learning more about this effective combination, feel free to visit The Temple's website[1]. At the end of our tour, we were told that now, after a few ceremonies, our hearts are more open, our bodies are cleansed and we're ready to go deeper and truly work with the medicine.

I felt this; I felt like I was ready for more. While feeling very grateful for the amazing insights, tools and healings I had already received, I knew there was something else, something deeper and bigger, that I couldn't quite put my finger on. I remember joking with a couple of friends when they asked me how I was feeling; I said:

"I am so ready, honestly at this point, I don't even care if I can't make it to the toilet. I'll just get my bucket (each one of us had a bucket next to the mat for a vomit purge) and do my number 2 there."

---

[1] templeofthewayoflight.org/information/ayahuasca-shamanism/

They gratefully replied, "Good for you and even better you're not sitting right next to us." That was my level of pure surrender.

I wasn't 100% sure about my intention. There had been something that had been stopping me from expressing myself, my knowledge, my truth. I didn't know where it came from or how to name it, and to be honest, I didn't need to dig deep into this and understand all the 'whys', 'from whom' and the twists and turns of this. I just knew it had been there for a long time, in my life. So, I thought I'd ask to get help with the fear of expressing my truth.

Then, just a few moments before ending the usual 'before ceremony yoga' class, I felt this deep shame in my body; it wasn't rational. There wasn't a story I would remember that happened to me, or a pose that made me feel ashamed. It was a deep old shame, stored as crystalised energy in my body. I had felt this a few months ago, and again, I thought this was gone. Obviously, not quite. So, in that moment, my intention became clear:

"Please help me with my shame."

During my first ikaro, I saw someone taking this ball of light out of me and washing it under a waterfall, washing and washing and washing. The rest of the ikaros in this ceremony sort of merged together; it was one big journey that had started just after receiving this cleansed ball back inside me. As I was lying down, waiting for my next ikaro to come, I started feeling my body, becoming really tall. Higher than the maloca, higher than the clouds, just very, very tall, and then very, very small again. As if I was a tiny ball. This pulsation kept happening for a while until I felt as if something left me. I was surprised and couldn't quite understand what this was, and as this was the time slot to go for our second serving if desired, I went for it.

I walked with the facilitator to the centre, and he asked me, as he always did:

"How are you?"

"Good", I said, "I'm good, but it was there, and the 'vjuuim', it left, and I don't know where it went, but I'm good."

I don't think I made any sense. I also think he was very likely used to people talking nonsense to him, but I could walk and talk, so I got served a small glass of another Aya, and he helped me back to my spot.

While my physical body did start to feel extremely cold, and I needed to put on all the layers I had brought with me and cover myself with the two blankets I had, I was able to come back to my vision and this sense of feeling really small. All of a sudden, I realised I was in the universe, a tiny, tiny ball of light in the infinite universe. I was a star. And I was dancing. And not only that, I was dancing while holding my legs in my hands, because I didn't really need them to dance.

And then, I hear this internal voice talking to me:

> "Look! Look! Look at yourself, you are dancing without legs. You're not your body, you're an eternal soul. You don't need to feel shame to express yourself; you don't need to feel any fear about what's on the earth. That's not all that is. You're this ball of light, that's who you truly are. Your life on earth is just one lifetime, just a very short period of your eternal life. You're free!"

It was incredible; I was laughing, internally and very likely externally too. I was doing somersaults, and rolling around as a ball in the universe. As a little embryo, in the infinity. The whole experience was with me, whenever I closed my eyes. It eased out as the ceremony ended, and I made it safely back to my Tambo. Yet, when I was falling asleep, I could still sense it; I was still somersaulting the universe with a huge smile on my face and a sense of infinite freedom.

Day 8

The next day we were dry fasting and in silence until lunchtime. Which meant no water and no food until 1 pm. I loved it. To be honest, sometimes I found the chatter took me out of my zone and contemplations, and I had to be careful in which conversations, and for how long, I engaged in order to not take anyone else's stuff on.

To clarify, this is completely my thing; as an empath, I often sense and get affected by what people are saying, not the meaning itself, but the vibration of it. I get stuck with it for a while until I consciously reconnect to my body, breathe through and realise it's not really mine. It's something I have constantly been working on, and it has improved a lot, yet it is still there, especially during this kind of healing when my energy is very open and vulnerable. So silence after this kind of experience was magnificent.

I was also still with it, on and off, feeling like this ball of light rolling around in the universe. I was in a state of not needing anything; I wasn't hungry or thirsty; I didn't need to talk; I didn't really think about the future or the past. Everything that was on this earth felt irrelevant, and nothing really mattered. In a good way. It was as if all the things, all the dreams, goals, and visions of the future, were not important. They were something far, far away, and I just was there and then.

Sometimes my mind came in for a moment, and I wondered:

"Is this ok? Or am I avoiding something here?",

"Just let it be, for now, just let it be and enjoy this flattening for a while, enjoy the bliss, you'll be back, don't you worry."

When the dry fast ended, I had delicious coconut water and a very brief talk with one of the facilitators, sharing how I felt. I mentioned that I didn't feel like talking to anyone or even eating, and her encouragement was helpful.

"Just go with it, there is no right or wrong, and you don't need to please anyone here."

So I decided to continue the food fasting until the next day's lunch. I did have some water as it's been really hot, and I felt like my body could use some of it.

I experienced something similar after one drumming evening, and I remember it was really hard for me to come back, to come back to work and to come back to this 3D reality. It's also something I have been working on - I can be ok on my own, in this solitude, in nature, with very little. Yet, deep inside me, I know this is not a vibration I'm meant to stay in. I know I'm meant to be on this earth to share myself with people, to create projects, communities and my family and not escape into solitudes to the mountains for the rest of my lifetime here. Don't get me wrong, I find it beautiful, and it can easily be some people's calling, that they're meant to be here. Maybe because it's more of a challenge for them. For me, it would be escapism, if I stayed in this 'space' for a long time. For me, it's a beautiful reminder of non-attachment, of how little I truly need to feel happy; it's a way to recharge and deeply connect vision on this earth; it's not a place to stay in. So my intention for that night's ceremony was clear:

> **"Please show me how to be on earth."**

The evening came by quickly, and I was ready to land; I was ready and excited to see what would happen. As my medicine was served to me, I decided to go for one glass only, even though the night before, I had a second and I could've had it this time from the start. It felt great to tell myself:

"I have enough. I don't need more."

The moment the group ikaro started I felt and saw myself coming back to earth. 'Swoop' a smooth landing. As I was back on earth, I was asked:

> **"What is it that you'd like here with you? What is your dream life? What would you like to create here?"**

And I went for it; I shared all my dreams for myself, for the planet, for humanity, and the visions of my vision. And these 'things' were landing one by one, all around me. Literally a whole new world was created on the earth. And I heard a voice saying:

> **"You can have it all. You deserve it all. As long as you are not attached to any of it. As long as you remember that none of it is really you, and you're this ball of light, this is just an experience you're having. And as long as you share this light, this message and anything you receive with others. It's all here for you to use. Use it gratefully, abundantly and without any attachment to it."**

"Bam!" there I had it. My curiosity led me to ask, how am I meant to share the light?

> **"Write, and you'll know. Don't force it, don't plan it all ahead. Let one thing happen that will lead you to another. Keep writing and sharing what you write. As the next 'mission' will come to you with ease, and you'll know. Trust it."**

I'll admit, my mind wanted to know more, but

"How will I know? How will I know what is the right thing?"

However 'the scene' ended. For a moment, I didn't see anything anymore; I was 'just a human' sitting on a mat in a room filled with people, listening to these strangely beautiful tunes and waiting for a song to be sung to me.

As I was receiving my first ikaro from Toni, I found myself in something that would be the easiest to describe as a dark forest. A very, very purple-grey forest, that felt safe and comfortable, with loads of tall softwood trees. There was this empowering fatherly essence all around me, encouraging me to walk. It felt very non-judgmental, supportive, unconditional, yet unattached.

> "You've got this, I have no doubt. I believe in you; just keep on walking, one step at a time, sharing your light, sharing your truth, humbly and you'll always be supported."

During my following ikaro, I kept bouncing in and out from the earth. It felt really grounding. It was as if the woman who walked through the jungle in my previous vision would turn into a ball, go into space, and then land back. But it was very quick; it sort of felt like those bouncy balls you can sit on and bounce.

> "Remember you're both, your thoughts can be spiritual, yet you're living on the earth, with the earthy things. Come to this place for inspiration, come often, but don't forget to live life on earth."

And I kept bouncing and bouncing until the whole vision faded off.

The next ikaro was different from my previous ones, as the others felt more like a movie scene I was watching when I closed my eyes, but this one was much more internal. Still experiencing it with my eyes closed, I felt as if all of my cells were being rewired. There were streams of colours and patterns running through my whole body. Not anywhere else around me, but within - from the toes to the head, to fingertips, behind my eyes, just like you'd see in the biology books, looking at the nervous system. But this one was much more interesting.

My nausea was very strong, however I kept burping only. Burping has been my way of clearing my body for a few years now; honestly, I burp during walks in nature, during yoga, during conscious breathing or dancing; this was no different. And it felt so good! As if my body was being completely reset.

The care and nourishment I felt when I was receiving my last ikaro are hard to put into words. It was this loving motherly feeling, which was also very grounding. It wasn't a fiery love, but rather a rooted care, safe and confident love. I felt a sense of completion, of pure grace and a very motherly touch. As well as a deep sense of knowing that it is my responsibility to pass this beautiful awareness onto the next generations.

It also made me truly experience the vibration of a healthy, intimate relationship (in my case, with a man). I got a glimpse of what is possible and what it feels like when two people who are committed to their own growth and continuously sharing the highest version of Self come together.

A lot of relationships around me, especially when growing up, weren't in a healthy balance, and I knew this was not what I envisioned for my future. Yet, I wasn't able to feel the new vibration of what it is. I could describe it in words, which is the first step. But it's truly our vibration, not our mind, that attracts. We are like magnets; what we generate around us, we attract. Until this moment, I wasn't able to tap into what I would like to generate for myself in this area of my life. Gratefully, this ikaro made me feel it, in every cell of my body, without any attachment to it. Without any thinking of 'I must experience this'. It was much lighter, yet much more rooted. It was a 'This is just how it is' type of feeling.

At the end of the ikaro, Laura said my name as she was giving me the closing blessing. This touched me on another level.

"She knew my name?!"

I was in this beautiful, open and vulnerable space and hearing my name was like getting a spoonful of vegan cream on my fluffy sponge cake.

She didn't speak English or Spanish, and the verbal interaction all of us had with the healers was absolutely minimal. They were with us during the ceremonies, 'doing their healing work'; they ate separately, and they didn't come to the group sessions. And honestly, it took me a really long time to remember their names. Four names, and I would get them mixed up, especially the ladies. Thinking:

"Vanessa, where were you until now?"

Tears of grace and humbleness began to roll down my face.

You can create anything your soul envisions as long as you're not attached to it

Day 9

Once again, the morning we spent in reflection and silence, fasting until lunch. It was blissful - to simply be and reflect more on what happened during the previous night. However, I also felt ready to talk a little and to start eating.

I find fasting (regardless of whether with Aya or not) is an amazing way to realise how little we actually need in life, it helps us reconnect our bodies and the simplicity of life. The first taste of food after a fast is like a party in the mouth. It makes us appreciate all the flavours, textures and smells. Then it's nice to keep the grace while enjoying the fact that we can eat, that we can actually have more, and that all of us are meant to experience this abundance within.

Similarly, with silence, it's crucial to contemplate, to stay within and to reflect. And then to share ourselves with others, as only in a context to something else, we see how much we have grown. We're all holding up mirrors to one another, guiding each other home. It's a reciprocity with everything that's alive, that gives our lives a drive to move ahead.

This was one of the group sessions I was excited about, and I felt fantastic after. I remember coming back to my tambo, and as I started writing something down, even more clarity landed in my consciousness in quite a practical way. It was a step that felt quite big and scary, yet I had known that feeling before. It was the same 'tingly fear' I felt when I made the decision to work with Aya.

Without trying to get hung up on it, at the moment, deep in my soul, I knew this must be the next step to take in my life. I told myself to let it be there, not try to figure anything out with my mind at that moment and trust that I'll know exactly when to make this next move. One step at a time, with peace in my heart, I was ready for the next day's closing ceremony and to start my integration time.

Day 10

This day, we had a meeting with the healers, for us to share where we're at and to be introduced to the process of the last ceremony. The last ceremony was slightly different to the previous ones, and we would also be receiving a protective blessing, to keep all the new energy within us. The rest of the day went smoothly, with the same schedule. However, everyone felt a tiny bit lighter, more open and more chatty.

We were also introduced to some ways to help us integrate. The diet we still need to be on for the following weeks and the conscious decision we should take while considering sharing these experiences with others. With some of these suggestions, I agreed more than others. In my opinion, not sharing our experiences creates more separation from people who haven't experienced working with medicine. It's here for everyone. However, how will you know, unless someone else shares the work? Of course, it's important that all the sharing is done honouring the method, the space and the healers. Of course, it's inevitable that some people will have their opinion and judgement on this. Well, so be it. That shouldn't stop anyone from sharing the beauty and shifts this work can bring to themselves and everyone around.

From the start, the ceremony was very peaceful and grounding. Yet, I'm not going to lie, there was a little part of me thinking:

"More? Is there more I can see and heal?",
"What if I won't see anything tonight?",
"What if this ceremony 'goes to waste'."

The ego was popping up again, wanting more, having expectations of how this all should go. Fortunately, the soul was much stronger:

> **"Look how far you have come. Look at all the goodness you have received and experienced so far. Enjoy the peace, ride this way of gratitude and enjoy the ikaros; maybe that's exactly what you need. Just to be. Without any visions, without any more conversations with the Self."**

And that's exactly how I felt. I was as present as I hadn't been before. Open and relaxed to be with what is. From that place, another beautiful vision arrived.

Do you remember the first scene from The Lion King? While the soundtrack of Circle of Life was playing, all the animals were introduced to their own habitats, joyfully coming together to greet the new Lion King. That's pretty close to how my first ikaros felt like. However, in my vision, the beautiful animals walking turned into people and then back to animals, then back to people who were dancing around in a circle while all of the animals gathered around them. Then the scene turned into dolphins swimming in the sea, while swimming with people and then back to the jungle. The spirit world and the physical world were united into one. We wouldn't have one without the other, yet they're one. Just like the Chinese symbol of yin and yang.

The second ikaro reminded me to have fun, to laugh for no reason, and to enjoy all of life. I was literally smiling from ear to ear as I was receiving this healing, and inside, I was bursting with laughter. Not at something or someone, just for the pure joy of it and to remind myself not to take everything so seriously during the times I do.

> "It is just one short lifetime out of many; we're all here on earth, remember?"

I started feeling really nauseous, and it became hard to sit up. I was aware this was what I had to do. With respect to the healer and because this is something I made a choice to be fully committed to. As I was sitting there, not quite knowing how to hold myself in this pain, I heard:

> "Some things in life might need a lot of courage and commitment, and you might not always feel supported by everyone. You might feel pain, or like you want to give up. Like there is no other way out. Just remember to stay... Stay with your soul's calling. Sit up in pain, in the middle of the fire, in your vulnerability and show up for what you have committed to; show up for what you believe in. With an open heart, humbly ask for help, and you'll always be shown the way through."

In my last ikaro, the beautiful motherly energy came through again. It was within me as well as all around me, encouraging me to be this vibration to myself & to others.

> "Remember this nurturing feeling. The way you would cover and hold a sweet newborn baby. The sweet and soft feeling, give it to yourself too whenever you get hung up in 'the doing'. And remember to share this essence with everything around you. In the way you speak to people and yourself, in the way you look into someone's eyes, in the way you step on the earth, in the way you water the plants, cut the vegetables, stir a pot of soup, draw a piece of art, create a post, write an email... in every way you are, remember to embody this way of being."

I felt sealed, falling asleep with peace in my heart and gratitude for all the experiences I've had throughout this time; as challenging and 'mind-filling' as some of them had been, they have always brought me back to feeling rather than thinking, to connecting to my own body, rather than to everyone else's, and to believe in creating a better world is possible.

Day 11

This was our last full day, which started with a small market at the Maloca, where we could purchase handmade items made by the healers and their families. After which, we got a tour of a permaculture centre called Chaikuni, which was right next to the temple. Those facilities were actually used for the Aya ceremonies in previous years. Recently, they were turned into one permaculture centre, where the space holders and volunteers taught sustainable farming - to the local communities and anyone who came to visit.

After a short tour through the gardens, we entered their maloca and were gifted a beautiful surprise. All the harvest from the day waited for us, organised neatly in a circle. There was so much care put into this, it really touched my heart, and made me tearful. It was there for us to try out and learn what each plant and fruit is for. What struck me the most were all the flavours and the abundance there still is in nature for all of us. Flavours I had never tasted before and only tried to describe, most of the time, it was:

"It's something like X, but not quite that. More like Y, but also not really that."

Recently, the centre started producing saleable products from the harvest - such as mosquito spray, lip balm, tea and cocoa beans. At the moment, these products are sold at The Temple, at The Permaculture Centre or in Iquitos. What they mainly focus on is empowering communities in Peru to create their own small sustainable gardens. You can find out more about their work at chaikuni.org

After lunch, we took group photos with the healers and had our last group sharing. I'll admit, I felt a bit out of it and irritated during that time. Part of me didn't even know what to share, yet there was so much to share. However, there was a difference in how I reacted to this, compared to how I would react to it previously. I just let it be there, telling myself,

"If you feel like sharing one sentence now and not going into it, do that. Regardless of what and how much everyone else is sharing, you do you, because that's the only way you'll be fulfilled. And then, allow yourself to let it be; don't dig into why you did or didn't share what you shared."

And I did exactly that; I shared what I did, with a very brief thought later on: I should've shared more and then I let it be until I felt called to share more with some people later on.

It became so clear to me:

> "Our life is very little about what is happening 'out there' around us, and much more about how we react to what's happening. That is what truly sets us free. That is what creates the new way of being; and that itself is then actually what changes what's happening around us."

Later, we went for a short walk to the local village, which consisted of a few small wooden houses on a small piece of land surrounded by the jungle. There, I learned about (and bought some) Macambo fruit seeds. These have a delicious nutty flavour and are filled with antioxidants and protein. And the big bonus - they were allowed on our post Aya diet - YAY. In a small, conscious amount, of course.

There it was - our last dinner. The healers joined us for this one, and towards the end, we took them off their seats for a little dance. It was interesting to notice how all of us have changed since we arrived. In some, you could really see how their faces had changed; they were much more 'alive', 'awake' and nourished. While with others you would notice the way they interact is different, more open, relaxed and confident. We ended up chatting till late into the evening; I think it was seriously the latest I had stayed up, during the last couple weeks. And I was in bed at 10 pm.

Day 12

It was one of those beautiful sunny mornings when I didn't need to use an alarm to wake up. The sun was shining into my tambo, and my only concern at that moment was that I needed to cover my crown chakra. We were told that at least 3 days after the ceremony, we needed to protect our heads from sunlight or rain, and I was a pre and post-Aya restrictions nerd. I even extended all the 'minimal' timings, just to be sure. So without thinking twice, I got up quickly, put my new hat on and started my morning.

We could ask for help with our luggage to be carried, and you know what? This time, I told myself why not?! My tambo is far, and this new version of myself is ready to receive. All packed and on time, I was waiting and waiting for it to be picked up - thinking, well, I'm practising patience here. After 15 minutes of practice, I decided I was done with this practice, and I'd rather practise my communication skills and trust in things to work out.

So, I left and adventured around, chatting with others while semi-looking for facilitators to organise this backpack-picking. Of course, it all worked out well, and I was grateful I got to spend some time with others rather than practising patience in my tambo.

Shortly after our breakfast, we made our way through the forest to the river, where the boats taking us to Iquitos were waiting. I don't think I spent as much talking with people throughout the whole retreat as I had done during the last couple of days. And it was wonderful. Sharing little nuances from our experiences and how we are feeling now, was a great proof of what truly is possible. It felt like now, once I'm out of this 'healing mode' I can actually socialise.

As we arrived at Iquitos, we slowly parted ways, squeezing in a last post-diet-friendly lunch. With a warm heart and loads of gratitude for the beautiful souls who were part of this journey with me, I was ready to leave. I was excited to start implementing this new way into my life, to write this second part of the book, to have some 'pura vida' (simple life) time at the eco-lodge, and to enjoy the hot weather before heading to the wintery UK.

I'll admit, a very little part of me, who, for a minute or three, would allow the ego to rule and question:

"Was this it? Did this actually change me, or am I still the same?"

I knew this was only the ego doing what it likes to do, and I was centred enough not to water this small seed.

I was aware that the real 'work' starts now. The cells of my body were 'upgraded' into this new being. For me, it is a state of inner peace, grace and trust. And now, it's about embodying and truly living this in my everyday life, in every breath and action I take.

The delicious fruits of this work will take some time to grow and be fully seen, yet I can tell you I never felt so committed, confident and trusting that the results will be epic and exactly what they need to be.

THE END IS THE BEGINNING

I have now arrived back in Devon, UK, where I have lived for the past 3.5 years, and as I got some sweet messages from friends saying 'welcome back', I reflected on this phrase, thinking, you know what, it's probably more like 'welcome forward'.

As I'm not really back, not the old version of me. To the one who was playing it safe, the one who would let the mind rule, the one who was seeing fulfilment and love in her morning coffee (saying it's just one cup), the one who would snack when she wasn't hungry, to avoid sitting with her feelings (happy or sad), the one who was so grateful for what is that she paused on her dreams and the adventure of being alive. For that version, I would like to throw a sweet 'farewell 4ever party'. Thank you for serving me, thank you for all the lessons (light and challenging) this version has provided me, and thank you for keeping me safe.

Now, I would like to welcome the new version of me - the one who is always sharing her truth, gracefully and with confidence. The one who knows herself enough to stay in her lane, regardless of what the majority of 'the world' is doing. The one who asks herself often:

"How is this serving me and the highest good of all right now?"

The one who is patient, connected to her breath and body and listens for the answers within. The one who is unafraid to make decisions without knowing where exactly they will lead. The one who trusts that when she (and all of us) live with integrity, grace and open heart, life will work out. The one who knows that the highest self, the highest power in this universe, doesn't want to harm us, make us suffer, or put bricks under our feet. It wants us to thrive, to live life on this earth abundantly. It's only up to us to see this, believe it and live it.

Reflecting on working with the medicine, my best ceremonies happened when I fully surrendered. When I said to myself, 'F* it, just go with this.' It doesn't mean it won't be challenging (just like sitting up on that soft mattress while being nauseous and wanting to sleep was), but it'll be worth it.

So I've booked my trip to Bali for four months initially. It's the trip I was about to embark on four years ago before Covid happened.

Yet, this time is different; this time, I'm not postponing it till 'everything falls into place' (which eventually didn't happen because Covid happened). This time I'm trusting that being aligned with my soul will make the rest of the things fall into place. And this time, I'm not going because 'I can't stand the way my life is'. This time, I'm going because 'I love where my life is, and this is part of it.'

As for you dear reader, thank you, thank you for letting me to share this part of my journey with you. To give you a different perspective on life and the infinite possibilities of being.

If you'd like to stay connected,
sign up for my newsletter at: vanessakrchova.com/newsletter

follow me or reach out on
Instagram @vanessa_krchova
Facebook @vanessa.krchova

Mucho amor

THANK YOU

xx Vanessa

Printed in Great Britain
by Amazon